Emotion and Imagination

Research and Imagination

Emotion and Imagination

Adam Morton

polity

First published in 2013 by Polity Press

Polity Press
65 Bridge Street
Cambridge CB2 1UR, UK

Polity Press
350 Main Street
Malden, MA 02148, USA

ISBN-13: 978-0-7456-4957-3
ISBN-13: 978-0-7456-4958-0(pb)

A catalogue record for this book is available from the British Library.

Typeset in 11 on 14 pt Sabon
by Servis Filmsetting Ltd, Stockport, Cheshire
Printed and bound in Great Britain by the MPG Printgroup

Epigraph taken from p. 120 of Bernard Williams' essay 'Janacek's Modernism', in his *On Opera*, Yale University Press, 2006. Used with kind permission of the publisher.

For further information on Polity, visit our website: www.politybooks.com

Contents

Contents

Preface

I have been thinking and reading about the emotions for a long time, publishing a loosely connected series of papers on the topic. This book began as a collection of these papers, which are listed in the bibliography. Then, encouraged by Emma Hutchinson of Polity to make a real book of it, I tried, and found new opinions developing and connections between old ones emerging. Still, the occasional whole paragraph from those papers has been incorporated. The result is an attempt to impose some structure on the variety of human emotions, as part I should make clear. Psychological research meets philosophical articulacy here, and while this book is clearly more philosophy than psychology, I have tried to be guided by the empirical facts I am aware of. See the references to experimental work in the notes. A readable and wide-ranging guide to what psychologists have discovered about the emotions is Fox (2008). There is an overlap with moral philosophy, too. I discuss many morally significant emotions in this book, and the reader might suspect that I think they are so vital to moral life as to *be* moral life. But as I hope the book also makes clear, there are better and worse emotions to feel, and many to choose between. I'm not sure that there's a circularity here, but it doesn't bother me if there is. On the nature of morality in general I am very sympathetic to the line in Copp (2007), though with doubts about how tight the unity to all the rules, beliefs, and emotions we take as moral might be. There is room for someone to put together a 'contractarian emotivism', developing the idea that what is right is what fits the moral emotions that we would agree to encourage one another to have.

I have learned from many friends and colleagues. Most of all from Peter Goldie, whose death in 2011 was a great loss to philosophy and a great blow to his friends. I have also gained a lot from discussions with Susanna Braund, Ronald de Sousa, Martin Gibert, Amy Schmitter, and Christine Tappolet, and had invaluable help from Chloë FitzGerald, Elliot Goodine, Jenny Greenwood, Nicole Pernat, Madeleine Ransom, Amelie Rorty, Juan Santos, Kathleen Stock, and two referees for Polity who may or may not be the same as any of these people.

... a reminder even to a philosopher of what should be done: ... to address, express, and restructure real emotions in ways that neither evade them with formalism nor degrade them into kitsch.

Bernard Williams, *On Opera*

Part I
The range of emotions

Refined emotions

We refine our emotions. From the rough sludge that comes naturally to us we distil the whole varied range of feelings that we can have, including some that are rare and delicate and some that are crude essential fuel. A central factor here is the relation between emotion and imagination. The central aim of this book is to explain the close link between the two, and how this allows us to have the wide range of emotions that we do, enabling us to direct ourselves towards emotions that fit our situations.

All emotion involves imagination. This is true of the basic emotions we share with mice, as well as the sophisticated and finely differentiated emotions that test the limits of our capacities to express ourselves in words and to relate to one another in complicated social projects. Or so I claim, and defend at some length. The claim may seem strange, since we think of emotion as common to animals of many kinds, while we may think of imagination as depending on human intellect and social sense. No – a fearful mouse imagines the dangers facing her, and people can imagine in ways that need little refined human capacity. The point can be put in a more cautious and less direct way. 'Emotion' and 'imagination' are both very loose words. Both can cover things that have little in common: the hope that your grandchild will behave herself on her birthday, and the foul mood with which you wake up on yours; the thought of how gold prices may react to a change in the property market, and the anticipation of how this spoonful of soup will taste in a moment. So in discussing them we will find ourselves tidying up their boundaries and making some arbitrary distinctions. The more cautious claim is then that we can draw the boundaries of emotion and imagination so that they fit together in a nice coherent jigsaw, one that is true both to the facts as we know them and to our experience as emoters and imaginers.

In defining the boundaries and arguing that the fit is a good one, I will appeal to imagination as well as to fact. That makes this an imaginative book on imagination: I ask readers to follow stories and consider the emotions they would feel in possible scenarios, and how they would describe them. (Of course, evidence, analysis, and argument are essential too. The notes at the end of the book have references to relevant empirical work, and to other authors and sources I am drawing on.) In imagining emotions, you will come to appreciate more how imagination and emotion fit. This method is inevitable, given my aim and given how little we know about many of the relevant areas. I am sure that people's fundamental attitudes are affected more by their emotions and experiences than by argument, so telling stories and evoking reactions gives me a chance of influencing my readers more deeply. But it does have dangers, some of which are brought into focus by following the method itself. In particular, the section 'Imagining invented characters: fiction and philosophy', in part II, discusses the danger that in philosophy and everyday life, as in fiction, we may imagine emotions that simply do not exist.

One result of distillation is the emotions that are central to our moral lives. Not that all of these are very refined: simple moral outrage is not that far removed from anger and disgust. The emotions of morality play a large role in the later parts of this book. To give a taste of those later parts now, here is a curious question about the persistence of sludge. Imagine a good person, who has emotions helping her generally to do the right thing. She is upset by the sufferings of homeless people, appalled by the self-indulgence of some young professionals, disapproving of cruelty to animals, and proud of her ability to balance her obligations to her family against the demands of generosity to others. What you might expect. Now ask whether there are less admirable emotions that could easily accompany, support, and fit with emotions like those I have listed.

It might seem that we would need to know a lot about this person's psychology, and perhaps a lot about the psychology of human moral behaviour in general, to say anything helpful. But consider the following list of soiled moral emotions: smugness, self-satisfaction, sanctimoniousness, and those associated with hypocrisy, priggery, prudery, selective moral blindness. There's quite a long list: they are epithets thrown by the rest of the world at those whose self-conception centres on morality. None of these describe emotions that our

person has to have. But they are labels that can be hard
for her to avoid, as they connect so closely to the valuable emotions I have listed. In later sections I describe
systematic ways in which morally focused people can
become prey to these emotions. You might take this
as undermining moral pretensions. I prefer to think of
it as a stab at how to take seriously issues of what we
ought to do and feel while avoiding some of the traps
that accompany being someone who thinks about their
responsibilities.

Consider our person's morally more relaxed cousin
('backsliding', 'irresponsible', she will say). Suppose
that, tired of being compared to his disadvantage with
his cousin, he describes her as smug. How can she defend
herself? It is true that she thinks that she has done the
right thing on many occasions when others have not. It
is true that she thinks that he lacks some qualities that
people ought to have and that she by chance or control
does exhibit. And are these thoughts not smugness? For
all that she may protest that she knows she is not perfect, and that she values him as another flawed human
being, she cannot deny that she thinks that there is
something wrong with him that is a lot less wrong with
herself. So the charge is hard to evade.

Hard to evade, but not impossible. The relaxed cousin
is pointing to thoughts that our good person almost certainly thinks. But thoughts are not emotions, so he has
not yet shown that she *feels* smug or self-satisfied. He
has a point, though. The emotions of a conscientious
person will generate a pressure, as I say below, to these
thoughts, and the thoughts create a pressure to smugness. More is needed for smugness, and I discuss this
extra content later, in parts III and IV. But there does

seem to be a facilitating relation between the emotions. Feeling disapproval of others and feeling morally satisfied towards oneself dispose one to smugness. Virtue has its dangers. There is more to say about this.

Imagining in emotion

When we fear something, we often imagine awful possibilities involving it. And at a more fundamental level we prepare for such possibilities and are alert for more. We look over our shoulders. When we are angry at someone, we have vivid quarrels with them in our minds. When we feel guilty, we create an imaginary accuser who points an imaginary finger. The imagining can take many forms, from vivid mental images to simple verbal thoughts to preparedness for perception and action. If you think imagination needs images, you may think that there is often no imagining at all. But on my approach to imagination, images and words are just one way in which we can grasp possibilities that might be important. This allows a close connection between emotion and imagination.

When we imagine, we represent something to ourselves: a fact, a thing, or a possibility. Sometimes we make a mental picture of it and examine the picture, turning it around and trying different approaches to it. Sometimes all we are aware of is thoughts about what we are imagining; sometimes we are not aware of anything, as when you are confused during your first walk in the southern hemisphere: you had not been aware that you expected the sun to travel clockwise, and that your sense of the way morning turns to afternoon depended on it. Imagination is a process rather than a result, something people do rather than something they get or experience. It is a process of searching for representations suitable for a specific purpose. Pictures and verbal descriptions are all-purpose representations and can be used in many kinds of thinking. The representations I am concerned with are purpose-specific. For example, you are holding a baby on your right hip while walking towards a step; you move your left hand over to steady the right wrist around the baby while changing your stride so that you come up to the step with the baby well supported. No words or pictures cross your mind, but you prepare for a very particular possibility, stumbling so the baby slips. I will say that you imagined this possibility and were apprehensive about it. You searched for ways of coping with the feared situation and found one, ending up in a state in which you were ready to notice the danger and ready to counteract it. This is why I am happy to assume that non-humans imagine, taking imagination to be a purposeful relation to a possibility, rather than images or words. A mouse imagines the cat that might be around the corner.

When we imagine, we are trying to achieve something with the representation, trying to get it to do some job. So if you are trapped in a building and thinking, imaginatively, how to get out, you mentally walk down one way and then another, hoping to find an exit. You are not representing the hallways and staircases in just any way, but making yourself attend to those features which are relevant to escape. The same is true if it all happens in words. You are going to a meeting where you expect someone will make an attack on your motives in supporting a project and you are considering how to reply. You think of various things the person might say and you turn them over in your mind, looking for flaws and openings for replies. You are not just thinking about what she might say but thinking of it in a certain light. If you find yourself representing her opinion as the interesting or informative one, you suspend that line and try another, which allows you to represent it as vulnerable or flawed. Almost all imagining has a purpose.

We can imagine actions as well as scenes and events. Of course we can picture what we intend to do and what might result, and we can describe these in words. But we can also form representations of the actions we are going to perform, as actions. That is, we can keep copies in our minds of the instructions we will send to our bodies if and when we perform an action. The standard example of this is planning to grasp an object of a particular shape. Before doing this you prepare by readying your control of your fingers to take the positions they will need. The fingers may not move and the muscles may not even tense, but the neural preparations for tensing and moving are ready. There can be some conscious awareness of this pre-movement, but typically much of it is unconscious. We not only represent the instructions we may send to our bodies, but we plan whole sequences of actions, together with anticipations of the sensations that will guide them and the feedback from muscles and limb-position sensors that may occur. We do this routinely. The easiest way to convince yourself in an intuitive unscientific way that this is so is to think of planning a complex action that will have to be performed quickly. You are beginning a ski run and you will have to turn at a particular pole, or you are planning to cycle along a narrow winding path, or you are preparing to dart your hand into a fireplace and retrieve a piece of paper that has fallen near the flames.

In cases like this, one has a sense of doing the action before doing it. Sometimes one rehearses the action mentally to get it more nearly right before launching the actual deed, and sometimes one just anticipates and then acts. In both cases it feels as if a model of the action has occurred mentally before the bodily action. Now this is one's sense of what it is like to act, which can be very different from what in fact happens. But there is also experimental evidence that we do form 'motor images', which are part of a complex integration of motor control, proprioception (our information about what our limbs are doing), and sensation.

Representations of actions are important for my purposes because they are at the heart of many emotions. You see a movie in which a child is being beaten and you have an impulse to reach out and shield him. Aggressive dogs behind a solid fence rush barking towards the fence as you walk by, and though you keep to your path you can feel your impulse to get away. A person with an abusive boss develops back problems, which are diagnosed as a reaction to her unconscious rage, and the suppressed impulses to violent action that it motivated. Of course you can represent an action for many reasons, not just in connection with an emotion. Emotions make us focus on the representation rather than the action because often, as in the cases just described, the action is not performed. In fact, the presence of a variety of representations of action, together with other representations, is essential to emotions.

Images do not make an experience into imagination. Nor do auditory experiences, nor do as-if actions. As I am using the term it is not imagination unless representations are being made and searched through in order to meet some criterion: the organism is doing something that makes it more likely that it will make some possibilities real and take note of other possibilities. Suppose that a very vivid image of your childhood home flashes into your mind, seen from behind the back porch at about two in the afternoon. You are not imagining it but remembering it or having a flashback of it. You wonder how you could have got up the steps and through the door pulling a toboggan, and you mentally approach the porch from various angles and see the outer and inner doors swing open in various angles and sequences. Then you are imagining, once you are doing something with the representations.

It is also worth pointing out that it is not a simple matter *what* is being imagined. Suppose that there was a picture above your bed as a child that you always thought was your grandmother. Sometimes you put yourself to bed and had no story or goodnight kiss, and then you would imagine that woman coming out of the picture, giving you a hug and whispering a short reminiscence from her life. You do not imagine her being grandmotherly, and in fact you have no information about your grandmothers, but just as being as she is in the picture, and being nice to you. You think that you were imagining your grandmother putting you to bed, but in fact the picture was of her sister, so you were imagining your great-aunt. Cases like this show that the content of imagination is often not transparent to the person who is imagining. This is also so when the imagining is unconscious. Suppose, to add to this series of imagination-describing imaginative exercises, that you are warned to be careful in dealing with the meter reader, who is short-tempered and potentially violent. The electric company truck stops outside your house and there is a knock at the door. You open the door, keeping it on the latch, and then have to look three times to see the meter reader, who is a small young woman. With a shock you realize that you have been mentally preparing for an encounter with a large middle-aged man. Between the warning and the meeting you have been imagining without knowing it.

Imagination, as I have been describing it, is in some ways rather like emotion. It pushes in a certain direction; it is going to a particular end. So the frightened mouse that anticipates carnivores leaping from unexpected places is imagining them, probably as inaccurately as we imagine many of the fates that await us, by setting in place a structure of responses to possible threats. When a plant moves, the mouse is prepared to freeze, smell, listen; her motor control is preparing to dash for shelter. This is like you in the meter reader case, when you half-open the door, prepared to see a heavy boot inserted to jam it open, and find your shoulder ready to jam the door shut, all without any images or words passing through your consciousness. The mouse and you are producing representations of possible situations, in order to be prepared for trouble.

Imagining is unlike emotion too, in a way that

---

suggests how the two fit together. We can imagine very specific things, such as the story that a bore may tell us for the hundredth time or the path that leads from the washroom to the back door. These are different acts of imagination, though someone could perform them simultaneously. You would, if you were dreading that Uncle George might corner you and tell you the story yet again and you were thinking of ways you could escape before he had the chance. Emotions directed at a topic will drive imagination of associated facts, possibilities, and actions. They have many of their powers by driving, pressuring, us to imagine, and imagination is important in part because it expresses and responds to our emotions.

Here is what I take to be essential to emotions. An emotion is a state which generates a range of representations on a given theme, usually with respect to particular objects. These include representations of actions towards the objects, representations of situations that might develop, and representations of results that might be produced. It is crucial that the representations concern both facts and actions. Emotions are like little belief–desire packages, with linked effects on how one interprets the environment and how one acts towards it. This is why a single emotion can serve as a short-cut version of a complex system of motives. The range of representations is held together by the theme. For example, a person feels horror at seeing a kitten killed by a dog. She represents ways she might have intervened, though she did not, and represents the kitten safe. She represents the actions of impulsively not observing the scene. She represents the scene itself, emphasizing its more disturbing moments. She replays her experience leading up to the event, comparing it to possible variations that might show it to be an illusion or a dream. Another person feels contempt for a colleague. He represents the colleague's actions in comparison with better alternatives; he represents crudely humiliating actions that he does not take, and more subtle dismissals, some of which he may actually act on. He thinks of how he would have done duties that he takes the other to have bungled, and he emphasizes unsatisfactory aspects of the colleague's performance.

Think of simple fear and anger, where representations of running away or attacking are combined with representations of the harm that the feared object might do or damage that might be done to the object of the anger. Some of these representations, for example those of means of escape and what one would have to do to take them, are very primitive and are similar to those of other creatures with which we share our basic emotions. We all have certain basic motivational packages that we use when the environment provides an appropriate theme.

In all of these we have a large range of representations, in which representations of actions and representations of situations are tied together by the theme of the emotion. Many of the representations are exploratory, such as various ways of escaping a threat, or hypothetical, such as kinds of harm that could come from a worrying situation. Many of them are anticipations of possible developments in the situation as it is, and thus represent dispositions to interpret the situation: the innocuous person who reveals a nasty agenda, the half-seen corridor that leads outside. There is no single representation that must accompany any emotion: a person who fears a stranger may imagine the stranger attacking her, or imagine herself running away with the person in pursuit. Many of the situations represented have little relation to the beliefs and desires that govern the person's deliberate actions: the terrifying driving test examiner is not really going to throw you out of the car or tell you that you are the worst examinee he has ever shared a car with. But they are part of what makes it the emotion it is, and they are also a large part of the reason that emotions are essential things to have. So one represents a situation as fearful by representing the bad consequences that could come from it, and in doing this one makes the threatening aspects of it stand out more definitely. This often remarked-on function of emotions, to filter information and options by making some more salient than others, amounts to the way emotions link representations of real situations to representations of various possibilities arising from them.

Seeing as

You can see almost anything as almost anything else, with a little imaginative effort. Here are some lines and shapes. What do they look like?

You can probably see a few faces, since we see faces everywhere. But it can also be a countryside seen from above, with roads winding around it, or earth-worms rising out of the soil. If I tell you the right story before showing it to you, you will immediately see it as a countryside or as worms. It can also be seen as a swimmer, with the tentacles of a giant squid reaching to seize her legs and drag her underwater.

The phenomenon is not confined to pictures and seeing. The first four notes of 'Auld Lang Syne' are the same as the first four notes of 'The Wedding March'. Try twisting the rhythm of either to make yourself hear it as the other. They have quite different characters as tunes (and one has associations of looking back in time and the other of looking forward). Tasting coffee when you expect orange juice will make it disgusting. And so on. Figures which are ambiguous in their perspective, like the familiar reversing cube, are particularly interesting, for in switching from one to the other way of understanding them, one is switching one's own position, as imaginary observer, from one place to another. So, we might say, in one of them one is imagining oneself to be looking in a different direction than in imagining the other. (In one of them one looks up at a base and in the other one looks down at a floor.) This is a point to return to.

One thing that happens when we perceive something *as* something is that many representations are produced, linked to the possibilities we are summoning. When you see that loop as a tentacle pulling the swimmer under, you also entertain a representation of her disappearing under the surface, and of the pull on her leg. You may well empathetically represent a struggle to free the leg or to keep your head above water. These are rather like emotions. Real emotions are present when actions of the imagining person are represented, for example the fearful desperation of someone trying not to drown. In other cases there are states that we do not have familiar words to classify. They can be complicated states involving many representations, rather like the torrent of associations produced by some works of art. Paintings, songs, and stories are not usually objects of literal perception-as, except in the trivial sense in which you see paint on a canvas as a winged horse. But they share the feature that in reacting to them we experience a host of shifting and competing secondary representations, helping to explain why we refer to our reactions as emotional, though frequently with a bad conscience since we know that these are not really surprise, relief, elation, but patterns of reaction that have something in common with them.

There is another connection between perception-as and emotion that is worth mentioning: the way that it affects the appearances of things. Sometimes this is trivial and obvious, as when seeing the moon's surface as a face makes the 'eyes' and 'mouth' locations more prominent while non-facial features recede. Sometimes it is more subtle, as when seeing an alley as a place you might be mugged makes the shadows seem bigger and darker. To anticipate an idea that will appear soon, a pressure is put on the appearances. It is as if the shadows were squeezed by the possibility that muggers are lurking in them so that their darkness oozes out to cover more of the scene. This can happen with accurately perceived scenes. You are shown the alley and told that it is a perfectly safe place but that some people are spooked by it, taking it as a place where muggers will wait for them on the way to their cars. You trust the assurances and you do not see the alley as dangerous. But you do see it as a somewhere that looks dangerous to others, and this 'seeing as seeing as scary' – seeing how it could be seen as scary – is enough to darken and stretch the shadows. The subconscious soundtrack for your perception moves down an octave and acquires some unresolved chords.

The imagining that is linked to emotions comes in crowds of linked representations playing out a story. But when we think of imagining we often think of a solitary representation, representing a single fact or containing a single image. In fact I suspect this is pretty rare. (It is usually supposing rather than imagining.) An image you summon to mind isn't like an enigmatic picture found on the street: when you imagine something, you give it a meaning, you take it to be a particular kind of thing, and you relate yourself to it in a particular way. Still, the imagination that is associated with emotions gives particularly rich mixtures of representations, and in particular includes motor images and plans of action. Moreover, in emotional imagination there is always a purpose, a story; the representations are never just imagined for their own sake.

I suspect that it is pretty rare that representations ever are completely purposeless. We can say 'suppose that there is silicon-based life on a distant planet', and consider the possibility without any pro or con or purpose. Or we can picture a planet that follows a figure-eight path around two stars which are themselves in a cyclic pattern relative to one another, just to see if we are capable of it. Or we can hold one hand behind our back and without moving it prepare to grasp various shapes or trace out various patterns, just to have the experience of doing this. (It is interesting that this sort of example is unusual among those that people use when discussing imagination.) These are very special human exploits, basic to curiosity-driven science and wonder-driven art, and connected with the fact that the emotions of curiosity and wonder lead to activities drained of some emotionally fertile aspects of imagination. But I take them to be exceptions, rare extreme cases that require a delicate background. And I conjecture that it is only because we have the richer crowds of representations that we can have these more delicately tuned ones.

Supposing is a very special, limiting, case of imagining. To imagine with freely multiplying representations, which link perceptual sensitivities and motor preparations, is to have an emotion. A dramatic and potentially misleading way of putting this is that imagination can be seen as a special case of emotion, or rather of some larger class which has emotion at its core. Perhaps emotion made thought possible.

Emotions and thinking

We describe some people as particularly imaginative. This always takes one particular form or another: one person is rich in stories, another in unusual practical options. This, rather than calculating ability, is often what we admire in people who are clever in various ways. And in fact the ability to solve mathematical or logical problems is often based on imagination, when a person comes up with their own route to a solution which can't be got in an easy mechanical way. Notice how original a lot of emotion-driven thinking is. Someone is jealous of their spouse's affection for a lover and takes creative revenge, filling the lover's convertible with fish. Another is suspicious of a salesman's motives, and besides watching her purse and her social identification number, she checks to make sure that the salesman has not implanted any recording devices on her. Neither is a routine or predictable action, but is the kind of thing that people do all the time when their emotions inspire them. And this is in accord with the biological function of emotions, to make us search for actions, and actions that will address problems of particular kinds.

To find ways out of our traps, we have to consider even unlikely ways of solving problems, and we must be receptive to even improbable patterns in the evidence. Thus a fearful person will represent to themselves, even if only fleetingly, quite ridiculous harms and elaborate ways of escape. An affectionate person will be sensitive to even minuscule signs of warmth in others. This is true of non-human animals too. A bird trapped in a house will search for routes of escape that it does not normally notice; a threatened dog will interpret friendly gestures as attacks. Humans, partly because we have language, can conceive of options of the utmost ridiculousness, and can interpret data in ways that no other animal would dream of. But then we have routines of reason, socially acquired and socially enforced, that tame these excesses, and all being well there is a balance between the creative imagination and the regulative intellect. But consider the other extreme, an animal with a single fixed response to a type of situation. When it receives signs of this situation, the animal goes into a state in which this behaviour and no other is produced. (Perhaps the situation is the proximity of a particular predator, and the animal plays dead; perhaps it is the presence of a suitable mate, and the animal goes into a courtship frenzy.) I would not call this an emotion, even though it may have some of the same neural underpinnings as terror, rage, fear, or lust. It does not connect in the same way with other reactions to situations, and it is not continuous with human attributes that explain actions in the same way as emotions do. We do, however, have a continuum rather than a dichotomy. Many animal emotions lead to a limited range of reactions, so there is a wide grey area between these automatic reactions at the one extreme and option-limiting, representation-forming emotions at the other.

Work by Damasio and others in the past twenty years has supported the striking observation that loss of the capacity for emotions is often accompanied by loss of the capacity for rational decision-making. Put more carefully, there are categories of neural damage such that patients injured in these ways have both a diminished capacity to experience emotions such as regret, fear, or worry and a failure to make sensible plans and decisions. (There is a lot more to say here. I should assure the reader that the general phenomenon is very well established, though its grounds and interpretation are controversial.) We should not leap from this to the conclusion that these emotions themselves are required for the thinking that is otherwise bungled. A more cautious way of putting it is that some central functions required for decision-making and planning are also at the heart of some emotions.

To be able to think well you need capacities that also result in at least some emotions from the standard list. That raises the question of whether there are emotions that have a direct connection with thinking. The obvious candidates are curiosity, and wonder, and the emotion-linked attributes of care and imaginativeness. You may wonder whether curiosity, and especially care, are really emotions. I defer talking about this directly, until the section 'Categories of emotion' below. In the rest of this present section, I discuss the role of these states, however we want to classify them, in good belief-formation, especially in science.

Imagine an extraordinarily able, well-trained, and malleable young scientist. From early on in her career she has been mentored by older scientists who not only are top researchers in her field, but also are pedagogically sharp and sensitive. The result is that she has a superlative grasp of research techniques, is aware of the live problems at the cutting edge of her subject, and has the patience and intelligence to do very good work. There is one flaw, however. She does not care about the subject. She has no curiosity. She wants a career, and she knows that with her background she is more likely to succeed by pushing some lines of theory than others, so she is capable of a form of scientific partisanship. But she does not find herself wanting the truth to turn out one way rather than another in more than this instrumental manner. She does not sometimes wonder whether lines of inquiry that are, with good reasons, disparaged by her research group might not in the end give important clues to the underlying processes she is investigating.

This scientist may well go on to do excellent work, and make significant discoveries. She may become eminent. But it is unlikely that she will lead her subject in radically new directions. Nor is it likely that she will be the one to find the new way ahead if current approaches stall, or to see deep subtle flaws in those current approaches, or willingly take her work in a direction that seems to her important but risks a lifetime of obscurity. She is rather like the child prodigy musician with rare skills and a marvellous technique, lacking only a love of music.

There are emotions she lacks, at any rate with respect to her chosen field. She does not feel wonder at the connections between facts that she can glimpse through the data. She does not feel curiosity about what scientists two hundred years later will have arrived at. Nor does she feel momentary scepticism – in everyday language a loaded attitude rather than a philosophical position – about whether current techniques can unlock the further secrets of the topic. The greatest defect is likely to be that her imagination has no emotional drive, so that while she can be counted on to be sensible and responsible, she will not represent to herself interesting unlikely possibilities. Wonder, curiosity, and scepticism are rather grand emotions with rather grand objects. But they are like the emotions that people feel in everyday life when they care what the truth is about everyday topics. A film star is charged with murder: is he guilty? We may have no bias either way but the evidence pro and con is tantalizing. We hope that a new piece of evidence will settle the matter one way or another; we are upset when a promising lead proves to be a hoax. I have no prefer-ence between the various hypotheses about why the Viking settlements in Greenland died out, but I would like to know which of them is right. I may feel vaguely disconcerted when a promising explanation turns out to be impossible. We feel all these emotions with respect to even more familiar questions too. Who keeps leaving half-filled cups of coffee in the photocopier room?

These are clear cases of emotion, because they involve mental events that occur at particular times, activate deep instinctive routines, and motivate us to courses of action. They connect with both the limbic system and the frontal lobes. We can be conscious of many of them, and may express this by saying 'I feel', and the feelings can be intense – joyful, bitter, exhilarating – or nagging.

Some of these emotions are linked to virtues – curiosity,

originality, caution – but they are not redundant given the virtues. The connection here has to be stated carefully. After all, our almost-perfect scientist had a large clutch of epistemic virtues, enough to equip her to do well in her field and make real discoveries. Even her lack of curiosity is qualified; she wants to find out the answers to many questions, though she wants the answers for reasons that are not purely epistemic. And all scientists and all inquirers of any sort are like this. We are motivated, most of the time, by the need to solve particular problems, and by the need to get ahead with our occupations. If we are in knowledge-gathering occupations, then the requirements of our jobs dominate our researches. And in our researches we show real epistemic virtues. So the scientist I described is not a monster. What she is lacking is subtle, and will show up only in particular circumstances.

The normal connections are these. We have practical concerns and information-gathering emotions connected with them: we are curious about the answers to questions of practical importance to us. To satisfy our curiosity we can inquire, of course; we can exercise our epistemic virtues in the required ways. We can also become curious about the truth of various propositions that arise in the course of the inquiry. But we can investigate these without being curious about them, since we can be guided just by our need to know the answers to the main question, and our curiosity about that is generated by the practical problem that made it important. Yet most people, in most practically motivated inquiries, do become intellectually curious about some of the questions that arise. And most inquiry can proceed without these secondary curiosities.

It is appealing to describe this motivation in biological terms, as following up scents, foraging, and exploring. A domestic rabbit, for example, put in a new environment, will explore it thoroughly, frequently rehearsing the routes that return to a safe location. A dog in a park will take stock of all the old and new dog smells, updating its database of who is in the neighbourhood. These are forms of curiosity, as basic an emotion as fear, anger, and affection. The most important feature of curiosity, for our purposes, is its persistent, hard to satisfy, quality. You may have acquired a perfectly serviceable belief, but curiosity drives you on to find a better one, or to check out the remote likelihood that it is mistaken. You may have explored all the lines of inquiry into a topic that you can think of, but in the middle of the night you find yourself toying with far-fetched ways of getting more information or applying different kinds of considerations. These are signs of curiosity, intrigue, and fascination. But see how narrow the divide is between these emotions and other less admirable ones: obsession, compulsion, nosiness, fixation.

Keeping mood and emotion distinct

A mouse senses the scent of a cat and becomes very, very wary. Circuits in the limbic system of the mouse's brain, particularly in the thalamus, begin to fire and the mouse becomes very alert to sounds and smells, especially those that might tell her of dangers. The activity spreads to another limbic region, the hypothalamus, leading to the release of adrenal hormones, epinephrine and nor-epinephrine. Her heart pumps, and her muscles become prepared to run. For this to happen, the mouse does not need information that the specific danger is a cat; she just has to be readied for a situation in which caution is called for and flight may be needed. She will startle easily, and in fact will be startled by signs of many other dangers as readily as by evidence of a large predator. She is in a fearful mood. It is a similar mood to the one you are in walking out of a vampire movie, when everything seems ominous and the traffic seems more threatening than usual. Your whole limbic system, which includes the hypothalamus, is acting much as the mouse's is, a tribute to the ancestral wiring that we share with other mammals. In your case, though, the sequence is more easily interrupted by sensory information and thoughts. We all feel fear.

But this is not the *emotion* of fear, not as I shall use the words. Although neuroscientists write of a list of primal emotions shared by all mammals, for me these are primal *moods*. An emotion of fear is what you have when you fear that your house may burn down (because, half-way to the airport, you think that you may have left a pot on a lighted stove element). Or when you suspect that the man who has rushed into the elevator is the killer whose picture you have just seen. An emotion has an object, and involves imagining scenarios around it. You are afraid that something in particular will happen. The imagining may be focused or diffuse, vivid or attenuated: it may be more or less similar to actual perception, and it may stay more or less concentrated on a particular theme. You may have vivid images of many kinds of bad effects from the cause in question, combined with impulses to do things to deal with them (leap out of the taxi, press the alarm button on the elevator). Or you may concentrate your attention on a particular bad consequence, the one that you consider most likely, and you may be searching your ingenuity for ways to minimize it. (The apartment is not going to burn down, but if the pot burns, the sprinklers will go off and damage the kitchen. Perhaps you have time to phone a neighbour, who just might be home and just might have a key.)

All of these are emotions, rather than moods, because in all of them you are afraid that something definite – imaginable, even if hard to put into words – may happen. This contrasts with pure mood cases in which you have a nameless fear of bad about to occur, or a terrifying sense of something unimaginable and awful lurking in your future, or even a vague sense of foreboding – 'something wrong here' – that puts you generally on the lookout. And they are emotions, rather than thoughts, beliefs, or desires, because in all of them the things you imagine are held together not by the immediate focus of any one of them (pushing the alarm button, the sprinklers activating, or whatever) but by the pattern and overlap of the pattern of all the things you imagine. Any one of them could be omitted and you would still be left with fear. The mouse *can* have the emotion of fear, as well as the mood. If she sees the cat and runs for her hole terrified of that cat, then it is an emotion she has. But it is harder to be sure that she does have this emotion rather than being in a terrified mood as a result of seeing the cat. These are easy to confuse: for it to be the emotion she has to be motivated to evade that very cat, rather than to general predator-evading behaviour.

Emotions often cause moods. Fear of a particular enemy may make you fearful in general. And moods are often among the causes of emotions. If you are in a fearful mood, you are more likely to become afraid that some specific trouble will occur. The paths are different in the two directions. A standard way in which a mood causes an emotion is that it makes one search, for dangers or mishaps or opportunities picked out by the mood. What one finds will often be the object of a corresponding emotion. (I have heard moods described as 'emotion hungry'; the clearest example is someone in an angry mood who would love an outrage to be angry about.) Emotions cause moods in ways that are less easily described as a pattern of thought, but which serve an obvious purpose. A person who is afraid of a particular threat will need to focus resources on that threat, and one way of doing this is to activate a basic mood which responds to that threat among others.

I suggest these two routes on intuitive grounds, without experimental evidence, for in fact experimenters are not careful about the differences between moods and emotions, and so have not done the work that might show ways in which they influence one another. But, for example, think of someone watching a skier approach an icy downhill run. She thinks of the run as very dangerous today, and wonders if the ski patrol are on duty. She is not worried about that skier so much as generally apprehensive about current conditions. Then she recognizes the skier as her child, and suddenly she visualizes all the bends on the run where one might fall, the trees one might run into, the moguls in surprising places, and has an impulse to rush down the run herself to give first aid, or to take another route and alert the patrol. (If she does any of this, her competent child will be really annoyed.) She even has a stray thought of wolves in the woods preying on fallen skiers, and then a fantasy of her own car breaking down in a snowstorm so that she freezes before she is found. The thought became an emotion early in the story, and is a general fearfulness by the end.

Suppose that the imagining you do when in the grip of some emotion is very imagistic. That will be a big part of what the emotion feels like to you. You are hammering in a nail and you remember to be careful not to hit your thumb with the hammer. That is just a useful cautious thought. But then you see in your mind's eye the hammer hit the thumb, and feel a wisp of the pain that would follow, and anticipate the yelling and jumping around. At that point the useful thought has become fear, and part of the fear is these images of the event and its consequences. Having an emotion typically involves a complex of imagined possibilities, imagined reactions to them, and imagined sensations, and these imaginations are much of what the fear feels like. (See the section on 'Pressure' below.) Sometimes the imagination is less vivid, less image-like. Then the experience of having the emotion is also less vivid. But it is still an emotion, and still is felt.

There are perfect examples of emotions, where they are clearly distinct from both thoughts and moods. A young scholar is going through a period of unemployment. No one wants to publish his dissertation, his articles are being rejected, and he is not being short-listed even for temporary jobs with mind-destroying teaching loads. He understands that his prospects are grim, and that he ought to consider other options. Perhaps driving a fork-lift for his father-in-law is not such a bad idea. And he describes himself as going through a bad time, considering himself generally a failure. He is inclined to see the gloomy side of a large variety of topics. He talks to a therapist about the depressive side of his mood. But he has hopes for his work. He has ideas about a little-known eighteenth-century thinker who is surprisingly relevant to the modern world. He thinks of journals which might publish his articles on his thinker, and plans to meet their editors at conferences; he has fantasies of an online edition taking the scholarly world by storm. There's a certain fertility to this: unexpected ways in which the research might take off keep occurring to him, though he admits some of them are pretty implausible. And throughout he feels despondent about his general prospects.

Though this is an unusual case, it is perfectly imaginable. Our scholar has a mood of despair, and in the midst of this an emotion of hope that his research will succeed. The hopeful emotion is deeply felt, but does not generate a mood of hope. He feels a hopeful emotion about one thing, which matters to him, but his mood is of hopelessness. (His gloomy mood may even lead him to think about disastrous consequences of the great success he imagines. Perhaps discovering this thinker was the worst thing he could have done.) Still, emotions dispose one to moods, and beliefs influence emotions, so the situation is not likely to last. The mood might swallow the emotion, and despair may reign over all his thoughts. Or the emotion might win, perhaps with the help of a little self-deception, so that many possibilities of success occur to him, and his mood lightens. Or the tension between mood and emotion might continue. Perhaps this is more likely on some topics than others: my impression is that many people have emotions about death that are disconnected from the moods that dominate their lives.

We often say 'emotion' when we are really talking about moods. There would be no real harm using 'emotion' as a general term for moods, emotions in the narrower sense, and various other states, *if* there was a clear general category here and we understood what it covered. But it is far from clear that there is. (I return to this question in the section 'Categories of emotion', below.) Any such category would be in danger of being a big, formless catch-all mess. So there is some point to being picky about words here, and not calling something an emotion when it is really a mood. We can ask whether when we describe someone as emotional we really mean that they are prone to intense sudden moods (though 'moody' has acquired a quirky little meaning of its own, something like 'quietly gloomy'.)

We also talk of some kinds of art, particularly music, as expressing emotions or inducing emotions in someone who appreciates it. But is this true? Suppose that a composer is grief-stricken because his mother has died. You hear the piece he wrote in this state (Mozart's *Symphonia Concertante*, say) and you are moved. Do you feel sad that Mozart's mother is dead? Or as if she had just died? Or sad that your mother has died? Or that mothers die? No, of course not, though these are all sad facts. You may feel something like sadness, though, something like the *mood* of sadness, a disposition to have sad emotions about things around you. Now all of this is very naïve, aesthetically. A more sophisticated line is that the music is sad in manner, in some very general way analogous to a person's manner, their posture and body language, when they are sad. So does the music seem to be behaving as it might if Mozart's mother had died??? No, no, no, again: it has something like the manner of a person in a sad mood, without attention to any particular object. As I will say later, the music is like a representation of the kind of pressure that a mood can exert on one's thoughts and actions, a pressure that other, quite different moods could also exert.

Mood and emotion are closely related concepts, though there are reasons to keep them distinct. One factor bringing them together is their association with a list of primary emotions: fear, horror, anger, excitement. These have the special feature that they have distinctive facial signs (postures, smells) so that they are easily – but not infallibly – attributed on the basis of simple evidence. That makes them quite easily learned: we can point to good examples and we can tell infants when they are afraid or angry, to train them in self-attribution. These facial and other signs are the same for the emotions and the corresponding moods: someone in a fear-filled mood will have a face that they might have if they were afraid that some particular catastrophe might occur. The distinction still applies to them, but it makes it natural that we should often ignore it.

Pressure

Think of someone who is afraid of a particular tiny harmless spider. He is afraid of all spiders, and as a result knows a lot about them. He knows that this species is completely harmless. He could pick it up and let it run over his hand if he wanted. But he doesn't want to; nothing could be further from his mind. He does not think that the spider can hurt him; he does not want it dead; he is even fascinated by it and would quite like having it near where he could have the thrill of being spooked by it. So his fear does not consist of believing anything definite about it or wanting anything about it. He would be a troubling case if we wanted to say that fear was just a kind of thought.

We ask the same person, who says he is afraid of the spider but does not think it will hurt him, what his fear feels like. He may tell us about sweating palms, jittery muscles, and an elevated pulse. But, importantly, he may not. He may deny all of these, or say they are no more present than usual. But, he will insist, it is fear that he feels. So what is this feeling business? I think

---

the answer to this is also the answer to why it is fear, rather than hope or panic or curiosity, that he experiences. Both come down to the pressure that the emotion puts on his thoughts, desires, conjectures, fantasies, and perceptions, in fact on his thinking in general.

The pressure works like this. Someone is afraid of an obviously harmless spider. He does not run away or attack it. But he notices where the door is; or he imagines how one might get an unwanted spider off one's arm. If there is a book on the table called *Thirteen Deadly Spiders* or *Rare Reactions to Spider Bites* he would notice it immediately and look inside. Images of really terrifying tarantulas may come to mind. He may find himself thinking what the best exit would be if one of them were to appear. If we give him a little evidence that the spider might be more dangerous than it seems, he will attend with interest, and draw conclusions from it hastily. The list of possible continuations is long and varied, and only some of it will apply to him. More of it will describe territory that he is near to, even if does not on this occasion occupy it: he may have no images of tarantulas, but if he had noticed the hairs on the sweet little spider's legs he would have. This is not so different from the state he would be in if he thought the spider was likely to hurt him. Then too he would be considering ways of escape and watching for aggressive moves; but in our subtler case these are not active plans and beliefs but plans and beliefs that he is inclined towards. Some of them he is more likely to have than if he did not fear. And some of them are present in attenuated form: instead of an intention a fantasy, instead of a belief a stray thought.

These are what I call the pressure that an emotion

puts on the rest of a person's thinking. When a person has an emotion, she is prone to think some things, wonder some things, be curious about some things, prepare and half-prepare to do some things, and above all attend to some things rather than others that would be in her mind if she did not have that particular emotion. Emotions are doing their job when they exert this pressure: the function of fear is to make us ready for dangers, of hope to make us seize opportunities, of despair to make us save our resources for better times. We become ready to resist or seize or wait, not just by acquiring particular information and intending particular courses of action, but by preparedness for possible developments. We need to be prepared for things developing in unlikely ways, depending on which unlikely ways our emotion is directed at, though it would be a waste of precious thinking resources to ponder them too explicitly and conceptually. So we come equipped, as all mammals do, with factory-set tendencies to some kinds of pressure. We humans can refine them to fit our needs, and indeed acquire completely new ones.

Years ago Ronald de Sousa defended a similar idea, with his 'paradigm scenarios' for emotions. The paradigm scenario for fear is that something may attack you or some happening hurt you; the paradigm scenario for jealousy is that some rival will get loyalty or some other benefit that should go to you. More recently a terminology of 'scripts' has become common. A script is a set of instructions, as in an actor's script, that specifies what a person should do, in this case a person in the grip of an emotion. There is a script for fearful people, for optimistic people, for jealous people. Scripts and paradigm scenarios capture the preparedness aspect of emotions.

But they miss their uncommittedness, the way that emotions are always departing from the details of the script: they are more like themes for improv.

In the second section above, 'Imagining in emotion', I described emotions as motivational packages, shaping actions as patterns of belief and desire do. But pressure captures the idea better. For any emotion there is a change in how likely many other states of mind are. Sometimes other states do not in fact change at all, but their likelihood changes. (The arachnophobic may not flee the spider, but is nearer to doing it, when his fear is active.) When a state is an emotion being in it makes it more likely that some changes in belief, desire, thinking, and perception will occur. These changes usually fall into some coherent pattern, so that the changes of one kind facilitate changes in the other. (Affection makes it more likely that you will think well of a person and their plans, and also that you will want to help them, and because you approve of the plans, you are not conflicted about helping.)

Emotions influence our beliefs and desires, directly or indirectly. A feeling of benevolence to someone makes it more likely that one will notice an opportunity to do them a favour. My formula for all this is that each emotion has a characteristic kind of pressure it puts on other states. And, in the opposite direction, some other states are characterized by the pressures that some emotions put on them – belief is intrinsically related to curiosity, desire to disappointment – in the familiar functionalist cross-dependence. Moods exert similar pressures, with wider, more diffuse targets. For example, someone in a fearful mood will be pressed towards beliefs about a wide range of dangers and ways to avoid or escape them, and will have perceptual and motor imagination drawn from the range appropriate to them.

Pressure makes feeling. The person facing the fearsome harmless spider thinks of large dangerous ones. Perhaps images of their hairy legs and rapid movements flit through his mind. He keeps track of where the spider is, always relating where it is to where he is and where he could be. He is open to information about the spider and its possible threats, though officially he thinks their likelihood is minimal. When a way in which the spider might hurt him crawls out of his subconscious, he pays immediate attention to it. And very importantly, there is a fundamental connection between pressure and seeing as. The spider man may see the little spider's legs as claw-like and its movements as attack-like. If the spider is trying to get away from him, he may see it as manoeuvring to get around behind him. He may see movements in the curtain as spider-like. None of this involves seeing anything that is not there, or even seeing anything wrongly. It is like seeing the twisting shapes as a struggling swimmer or hearing 'Auld Lang Syne' as 'The Wedding March'. It is primarily selective, making some aspects of what we perceive stand out more than others.

This is an important clue to how emotions, and moods, have perception-like feelings. Besides their effects on our bodily sensations – whose presence I think many writers overestimate – and their prompting of images specific to their themes, there is the effect they have on all our other perceptions. They re-develop the pictures that are already there, overexposing some parts and underexposing others. I suspect that this is part of the reason why people associate bodily sensations with some emotions. The heartbeat that you are often marginally aware of is perceived as throbbing as a feared event threatens to occur; the regular rhythm of your breathing becomes something you are aware of as you anticipate controlling it to meet a physical challenge; the long exhalation that you often make is taken as marking the point when anxiety turns to relief. So emotions can affect what our felt experience is like even if there are no specifically emotional feelings, by changing the meaning and emphasis that we impose on our pre-existing experience.

It is also a clue to how emotions can be unconscious, and more generally how we can fail to be aware of our emotions. In the first place it is not easy to be aware of changes in how likely one is to do or notice something that one isn't doing or noticing. And although the pressure that results in these changes in likelihood will often result in changes in perception too, these are changes in kinds of perception that one would have had anyway. When someone has an unconscious emotion of resenting his friend's success, he finds good reasons to think the friend's accomplishments as less than they might appear: reasons which would have some weight whatever the motive for thinking of them. And when he notices the moment of smug self-satisfaction that flickers across his friend's face, well, the smug look really was there, and it might have been just by alertness and social acuity that he noticed it. So although all the signs of resentment are there, it takes an effort of interpretation to put them together and see them as results of a single coherent pressure.

Besides seeing as – and any actual imagistic content, including anticipations of pain, discomfort, pleasure, satisfaction – emotions and moods put pressures on thinking. There is a conceptual and an experiential side to this. On the conceptual side, emotions make some beliefs and some patterns of thinking more likely. And they push us towards evaluative judgements, in ways that connect with the themes of parts II and IV. It will be important then that the emotion and the judgements it pushes towards are different. Fear cannot be simply the evaluation of something as dangerous, let alone the perception of its dangerousness, since one can fear harmless things while knowing clearly that they are harmless.

On the experiential side, there is the rhythm of the thinking that is prompted by the emotion, whether it is frantic or measured, leaping from one issue to a distant one or following a predictable path. There is the sense that a line of thinking is constrained or free to wander into unforeseen territory. We can be aware of some of these structural effects – what kind of thinking it is – and thus know that our thinking is rushed, frantic, measured, deliberate, or jagged. It is interesting that these are also adjectives that we often apply to music. I think it is one source of the popular idea that music is inherently emotional (or mood-laden). It does not support the idea but diagnoses it. Given a piece of music thought of in terms like these we can find emotional episodes which would produce thinking – trying to remember the way out of the trap, following the signs of a familiar way home – that would have the same structural qualities. But we could find very different emotions which could pressure thinking in the same way too. The music of thought is a frequent effect of emotion, but does not characterize either music or emotion.

Categories of emotion

Love, depression, anger, curiosity. These are all very different states, and influence our actions in different ways. If we lump them all together as 'emotions', we are ignoring basic differences. But keeping them separate would be easier if we had some substitute concepts, to divide all the things loosely called emotions into a better classification. These are hard to supply.

We have not always used the word 'emotion', not even in English. Some three hundred years ago people talked of passions, sentiments, emotions, feelings, and affections, and used all these terms to cover wide classes of states. 'Passion' and 'affection', no doubt influenced by stoicism, suggest factors that we are passive in the face of, or affected directly by, by-passing the control of rational volition. 'Sentiment' suggests the influence of opinion or other belief-like states. (The *Oxford English Dictionary* gives a citation from 1702: 'Now there is an exact Parallel to be drawn betwixt one and the other, according to the Sentiment of several of the Ancients.' It is like the use of 'feel' in 'I feel that you are wrong'.)

A sentiment is a judgement-linked long-term emotion, such as disapproval, and in this use it has been revived by recent authors giving the emotion-centred accounts of morality discussed later. 'Emotion' suggests the moving influence of desire-like states. In contrasting sentiments to emotions, we might think of the contrast between fear and anger, taking fear to focus on a belief that something will harm one, and anger on a desire to do harm to something.

That is suggestive, but the details are confusing. I cannot give you a formula capturing the difference between emotion, passion/affection, and sentiment that fits the usage of David Hume, Adam Smith, or other such authors. (This may simply reflect the shallowness of my scholarship.) In fact the same state can be called a passion, a sentiment, and an emotion by the same author. The contrast between fear and anger shows some of the problems. Fear has an element of desire as well as an element of belief, since it involves a disposition to get away from the feared object or to prepare defences against it. Anger has an element of belief as well as one of desire, since it involves the thought that the object of anger has offended or deserves punishment. Both of them can overcome carefully thought-out plans, so that part of our personality can be passively affected by them. And of course even without the encouragement of stoic philosophy we can often do what we think we should in spite of fear or anger. The variety of commonly used labels for emotion in older English seems not a rival classification of states but an expressive device for stressing the aspect of any state that is most relevant to some particular emotional incident for some purpose.

The distinctions I am looking for would cut across the

---

contrasts between moods and emotions. For example, we can have an emotion of anger and be in an angry mood, and we can have an emotion of depression – be depressed that something particular has happened, perhaps that your book got a terrible review – and we can be in a depressed mood. But if anger and depression are not just very different states but fundamentally different kinds of state – as I am convinced they are – then both the mood and the emotion of anger will differ in that way from the mood and the emotion of rage. Still, the distinctions between emotions, moods, and character traits are helpful in the quest. One significant fact about them is that they each mark several contrasts at once. Moods lack determinate objects but are also typically passing, and while episodes of emotional feeling are typically quite short, one can have an emotion for a long time (think of hate or hope or resentment). Traits of character lack objects, like moods, but they typically last for a long time and are used to explain a very large range of actions. Of course each of these labels covers an enormous range of states, including deeply different ones. They are like the everyday words 'bug' or 'dirt'.

The contrasts that made people in the past speak sometimes of passions and sometimes of sentiments or emotions cut across other ways of classifying our states. This is naturally taken as part of a four-way distinction, between emotions, moods, states of character, and virtues. Someone may be in a courageous mood – she'll stand up to anything – though there is nothing in particular she is being brave about, and someone else may be feeling the emotion of courage about some particular threat. That's his emotional reaction to the situation. Yet another person just is a brave person as a matter of character: it takes a lot to intimidate her, though there is nothing that she is being courageous about at the moment. A fourth person does a courageous act, without feeling courage or being by nature brave. That's the virtue of his act. A fifth often does courageous acts, but only when it is courage that is called for, rather than prudent retreat or patience. That's her personal virtue, and thus a trait of character that is also a virtue. Many of these states involve dispositions to other ones: someone with a brave character is disposed to brave emotions, someone with the virtue of courage has to have a brave character. (But a person disposed to brave deeds need not often be in a courageous mood.)

Cross-cutting these distinctions, there are those between passions, sentiments, and emotions. To see this, contrast two cases of anger. At one extreme is the impulsive but understandable ire of Irina, who is the recipient of a sexist remark by an immigration officer. ('You're coming here to do a Ph.D? In glamour?') She stews for just a moment, then hits him over the head with her laptop case. In that moment she has a hard-to-resist impulse to strangle him with her bare hands, and imagines with pleasure his purple face as he struggles to breathe and apologize. This is anger as passion. At the other extreme is the deliberate and carefully placed anger of Fabius, who loathes the tax structure of his country for the way it fosters inequality and its tolerance of evasion. He places himself carefully, gaining accountancy and legal qualifications, and works his way upwards in the tax department, until he is in a position where he can identify the files of the thousand extremely rich people who pay the least taxes. He manages to have half of these audited in ways that reveal their unreported stashes, and he releases the names of the other half to Wikileaks, with figures that reveal their callousness. When a friend asks him why he directed fifteen years of his life to this act, he says, 'Anger, simply anger: I couldn't let the bastards get away with it.' That is anger as sentiment, no less a deeply felt emotion but with more links to worked-out thought.

Irina's anger is immediate and violent while Fabius' is slow and subtle. So there are differences in intensity and duration. Not that Fabius is any less angry than Irina. The difference I want to focus on, though, involves the experience of anger for the two people. Irina's anger experience is revealed in definite pictures of the havoc she could wreak on the smug fool in front of her. Fabius has no pictures in his head, and when dealing with billionaires he has no trouble behaving in a polite and professional way, though the occasional ironical smile crosses his face at protestations of what the oppressed billionaires cannot afford. Yet through all of this his anger is intense and motivating. And it is strongly felt, though he is not aware of it every waking minute. He thinks a lot about ways the super-rich might be brought to account, some of it in practical terms and some of it as idle fantasy. But even in the fantasy there is always a direction. His thoughts about other matters can be interrupted or side-tracked by these angry thoughts, and he has to think hard to see the problems in really quite unlikely schemes for bringing cheaters to account. When he thinks of smug rich people, he usually thinks – joined to this, as part of the same thoughts – of children stuck in poverty and parents struggling to bring up children. These patterns are a constant background score to his life; they are part of what it is like to be him.

The difference between passion-type anger and sentiment-type anger is emerging as a difference between the kinds of pressure that they apply. Passion produces impulses to immediate action out of reactions to immediate events, and sentiment produces long-term plans out of an evaluation of the general situation. It is not a sharp distinction, obviously, but it applies to moods, character traits, and virtues as well as it does to emotions closely conceived. There are two cross-cutting distinctions in play, one between passions and sentiments – or what we may use these traditional labels to mean – and one between moods and emotions. So there are four possible combinations here. *Mood & passion*: a good example would be being in a furious mood, which hungers to generate an angry emotion as soon as it finds a suitable object. *Mood & sentiment*: here we should put being depressed or paranoid, strongly inclined to think of your own life or social life in certain terms. *Emotion & passion*: being furious at a particular event, as in Irina's case. *Emotion & sentiment*: anger that is supported over a long term by a thought-out policy, as in Fabius' case.

There are intermediate cases. Consider, for example, a standing annoyance at colleagues for their incompetence, as much a readiness to find cause for complaint as it is a reaction to any particular misdeed or bungle. This would be a mood on the sentiment side, but definitely on the emotion side of depression or paranoia. Or consider the worried mother from the discussion of mood and emotion, as her ominous sense that this is a day when bad things could happen is beginning to focus on skiing and starting to interact with the concerns she has had about this particular resort's safety procedures. That is right is the middle of the array, more of a mood than her later emotion of fear for her child on the slopes, and more of a sentiment than the ominous feeling from which it grew.

There is a dilemma here for a project like this book. My aim is not primarily about finding the tighter categories that might serve us better, but I do not want to perpetuate the old sloppy usage either. Moreover, good categories should pull together the everyday explanations we give and the physical facts underlying them, and that is too large a target now. My solution will be often to speak very loosely of emotion to refer to any state that exerts a pressure on other states that has a focus we can describe in propositional terms. I will try to keep an emotion–mood contrast generally in mind, though, and to some extent a passion–sentiment contrast, especially when they are relevant to finer distinctions I am making between particular emotions. In the end we should have some broad, vague, general terms and some extremely precise ones. This is the way it should be: we need words like 'colour', for all their vagueness (is grey a colour? is transparent a colour?), and we also need words like 'mauve' (not to be confused with violet or puce) and 'saturated'.

Part II
Imagining vile emotions

Imagining what we shouldn't feel

B: *Did you see this news report of a mother who cracked when her baby cried through four nights in a row, and shook him till he had to be hospitalized? You're a parent: how can anyone behave that way to their own child?*

A: I've got pretty desperate when the beloved infant got me up five times in a night, but never to that point. I've always thought it remarkable that parents crack so rarely. But yes, I can sort of imagine what that mother went through.

B: *You mean that you can find baby-shaking in yourself?! And you've taken care of my kids. Please explain.*

A: Well, here's what it's like. You really need your sleep on a hot summer night and there's a window open somewhere in the house. A single mosquito gets in and that persistent humming – I believe it's pretty exactly a tuning A – gets nearer and retreats, then is ominously silent. You toss around in bed and listen for it. This goes on for hours. And then suddenly you jump up and scream, and run around the room with a pillow in your hand, trying to swat the creature. I think it's like that.

B: *Your own baby? A mosquito? Come on.*

A: You've got to get into that frame of mind, desperate for sleep. So suppose that you're in love with a hyper-vegan and if you so much as threaten that mosquito she'll lose faith in you. So you lie there restraining your fury, for hours and hours, and then finally it erupts like lava, and as you run around trying to murder the little beast, you know that it's just what you mustn't do, that she'll hate you for it, that you're threatening everything that matters to you. Haven't you ever had an itch that you weren't supposed to scratch, but couldn't resist? Once I cracked a cast with a hammer, and had to have my arm re-set. I knew at the time it was stupid.

B: *I don't think I want to go where you're leading me. So it's just by the grace of God that we haven't all assassinated our children? Most of us have decency and control and a few do not. I can't even imagine what it is to be like that, thank goodness; that shows how different we are.*

A: I can give you other models. There's uncontrollable laughter at something ridiculous during a funeral. There's throwing a bottle at the television when your team loses. There's blurting out something you've been wanting to say for years but know you really shouldn't. These all are emotionally similar, though they're different emotions. It's the same sort of feeling.

B: *Now I'll be afraid of thinking about mosquitoes when my baby cries. Some emotions just are very different from others.*

Imagining other people's emotions is an everyday occurrence. It is a central part of understanding others – their motives, their actions, their feelings – which we do many times every day, often without thinking about it, in our routine interactions with them. Sometimes we fail to understand, too. Either we attribute the wrong emotion or motive to someone, or we are just baffled, and we do not know why someone did something, or what the person was feeling. I shall be concerned with understanding people's emotions, and in particular with emotions such as empathy and sympathy where one person feels an emotion that relates to another person's emotion. In that particular case we often feel baffled, having no grasp of what someone else might have felt. Sometimes we do not want to know someone's emotion. We can feel this for the emotions that lead people to awful or evil actions. This can be summed up in a fast and sloppy argument as follows: A decent person cannot understand why someone did an evil action. For to do so she would have to feel empathy for the evil-doer. But we should feel condemnation rather than empathy for evil, and someone who did feel empathy would have some form of the same emotion, the hatred, rage, or obsession that brought about the act. A decent person could not feel this while remaining a decent person.

This is *not* a convincing argument. I shall be working to show quite how wrong it is. But it does capture a barrier we can feel, that stops us from getting too psychologically close to people we are appalled by. We feel that if we were to get an intuitive, not-just-theoretical, understanding of them we would to some degree become like them. And we would rather remain ignorant than have this happen. I think this danger, which we all feel, is exaggerated, for reasons that are linked to the main themes of this book. So one of my aims is to soften the barrier: what's on the other side is not so dangerous. Keep, then, questions like this in mind: how can we empathize with hatred without hating?

Imagining minds:
emotions and
perspectives

We often imagine people's state of mind. Suppose that you see someone about to get on a bus, then pausing, stepping back to the street, and looking around on the ground. You may wonder why this person is acting this way, and you are likely to run little scenarios through your mind. She looks puzzled: perhaps she noticed that she did not have her hat, sunglasses, or purse. Perhaps she had seen some money – or a diamond necklace – on the ground and went back to check if it was worth picking up. But she does not look distressed, so she is unlikely to have lost something valuable. You may not have enough confidence in any of your guesses to believe that these are her thoughts and motives, or to use them to explain her actions. You may even be sure that no such story is the case, so that the scenario is just a fantasy to amuse yourself. Whatever your attitude, you are imagining a state of mind.

Imagining people's minds is central to the texture of human social life. We frequently imagine our own minds, indeed our own imagining: when you responded to the instruction 'Suppose that you see someone about to get on a bus . . .' you imagined yourself wondering about the person's motives and coming up with various scenarios. You imagined your own curiosity and interest. We frequently imagine other people imagining us, as when, for example, we go out of our way to prevent someone even supposing that our motives might be exploitative or seductive. We do a lot of very complicated imagining of one another's minds, quite routinely, without remarking on it. And very often the imagining is extremely vivid. It seems very real to us. Suppose, for example, that you are comforting a friend who is recently bereaved and extremely upset. His feelings, as you imagine them, are for you just a definite fact about the situation. They are among the things you have to take account of in deciding what you should do.

What is it to imagine an emotion? Well, you may say, one thinks of having those feelings that push you to act in those ways. But that's too thin. Someone might think about the feeling and the urges without imagining them. I describe to you a peculiar made-up emotion I call 'worminess', in which the person wants to tunnel through the ground eating dirt while having characteristic sensations of blood being circulated by several hearts. 'OK,' you say, and you think about worminess for a moment. Have you imagined being wormy? Of course not: you probably could not get any representation of the urges into your head, and I gave you no grip on what the sensations are like at all. But you did *think* about the supposed emotion for a moment, graciously granting that I was talking about something real. So instead we may go the opposite way, suggesting that to imagine an emotion one has to *have* something like the emotion. That's in danger of being too thick. Imagine you are told of someone who fell over a cliff and lay with multiple injuries till they died of shock and thirst. You can begin the task, getting a sense of the terror, despair, and frustration that must be involved. You might say, 'I can't imagine anything more horrible' (though actually you could, sadly). But surely what went through your mind in the thirty seconds you were imagining the victim's feelings falls far short of what the victim went through. You may have forgotten it a day later. Still, you may have been imagining the experience as well as anyone who hasn't undergone it could. If total accurate reproduction is required to imagine an emotion, then we rarely if ever do it: we rarely experience all of what it really is to have that emotion, without actually having it. We have to acknowledge both how vivid and intuitive our grasp of one another's emotions often is, and also how incomplete, fragmentary, and inaccurate it can be.

The problem is solvable. We can hold onto both vividness and incompleteness. Consider some parallel cases. You can imagine the tininess of the earth in relation to the whole galaxy, or of your life in relation to the age of the earth, in both cases vividly but also very incompletely. You can imagine a labyrinthine building so complex and irregular that you lose track of its structure after half a dozen corners. For that matter you can imagine your mother's face, though you fail to represent the placement of every hair and the shape of every crease. In all these cases, in fact most times when we imagine, we represent something in a way that is directed at a given purpose and because of that includes only details of it that are relevant to the purpose, indeed usually only a selection of these. The images and other states of mind that the imagining bundles together may not be enough to pin it down uniquely. You imagine your mother's face though nothing you bring to mind would distinguish her from your memory of her mother at the same age. But it is your mother you are imagining and not your grandmother.

This is a topic that has been much discussed in the philosophy of art, under the banner of what makes a picture be a picture of one person or scene and not of another. You can have a cruel caricature of your mother's face, a sentimental glamorization, or a few well-chosen lines on a scrap of paper. All can be pictures of her, because the fact that she is the origin of the image is a central cause of the ways that the image can serve your purposes, and because, to link up with a theme of part I, it is interaction with your mother that the pictures facilitate. These purposes can be very varied, but they all require that it be a picture of her. And even the most accurate portrait is not really much more similar to its subject than the kettle on the shelf is. (Just ask any passing Martian.) Similarly with emotions. When one person imagines another person's emotion, the imagining is itself an emotion. It's an emotion *of* the other person's emotion, depicting it, and like a picture it is a very partial and selectively accurate depiction.

I said that to imagine an emotion is to have an emotion, one that is of its target. That sounds startling, and some distinctions are needed. Consider what it is like to be in the presence of someone who is dramatically nervous and anxious. She looks in random directions for threats or facts she should have noticed; her speech is broken with pauses and sudden changes of conversational direction. You do more than just apply a verbal label or note the behaviour. You try to get a sense of what her state is like. To do this you shift your own attention to the objects of her attention and concern, trying to shift around in time with her; you attend to the actions that she considers doing, and in doing this you at least consider what would be involved in doing them. Doing this is picturing nervousness, her nervousness, to yourself. It would be hard to do it without feeling at least a little bit nervous yourself. But even without saying that, you have to admit that you are experiencing an emotion, an emotion of depicting someone else's nervousness.

This is true in other cases too. Suppose that you are walking down the street and a perfect stranger is suddenly furious with you. (The story doesn't matter; you might have inadvertently jumped to the front of a long queue.) You feel a variety of things: alarm, fear, puzzlement, distress. And anger, both the stranger's anger at you and your angry-defensive reaction. Your sense of the stranger's anger tries to find out what its objects are (can it really be me that he is attacking? what have I done? what might he do to me?). And it tries to determine that it really is anger rather than craziness or acting or whatever, exploring the kinds of behaviour to be expected of each (and thus also exploring what the stranger might do next). Suppose the fury rises and you fear real physical assault. Then you explore possible escapes, defences, and counter-attacks. These are parts of the emotion of fear, but it is a fear that is tuned to the anger it responds to, and as your sense of this anger changes so does the fear, picking different objects and possibilities. So here too the vivid apprehension of someone else's emotion itself has the characteristics of an emotion. (Different people can experience incidents like this differently. For some, fear or defensiveness will dominate, and the sense of the other person's anger will be in the background. Others will first of all feel the other person's anger, as anger, directed at them, and will have a secondary feeling of searching for a response to it.)

There is a general pattern here. Imagined emotion is emotion, or, to put this more carefully, imagining particular people's emotions at particular times generates emotions related to the imagined ones in systematic ways. These are not necessarily the same or even similar emotions, though they can be, but emotions *of* their targets and related to them. For there almost always is a reason why we imagine someone's emotion, and we can't further that purpose without taking the imagination in some directions and not others. There is a pattern of representations of facts and actions, a selective emphasis on things perceived and options considered. And that's an emotion.

Come back now to the incompleteness of imagined emotions. When one person imagines another's emotion, she represents some aspects of the emotion in ways that are themselves emotional, and typically these are parts that impact on her own life. Other aspects are left unrepresented, and yet other aspects are represented in words or in some other conceptual means. All of these can be accurate or inaccurate. But the whole is inevitably incomplete, and in particular the emotional imagination must be incomplete. It can still hang together as a depiction of the other person's emotion. The question of accuracy remains, which I return to in the section 'Misimagination'; it is important because of the central question whether vividly imagining a vile emotion is itself a vile thing. If we allow inaccuracy as well as incompleteness, then the task becomes trivial. We might as well imagine an ice-cream and count that as imagining hatred. So once we realize that all imagination is incomplete, the question of what distinguishes an accurate incomplete imagining from an inaccurate one becomes vital.

Imagining a point of view

You are imagining the emotions of a particular person in a particular situation, for example a bereavement which is both a blow and a relief. So you are trying to grasp what it is like for the person now. (You can behave sympathetically without a good sense of how shock and deliverance combine, but I am supposing that you are really trying to grasp the situation.) This is more than just applying the words 'bereavement', 'shock', 'relief', since you also have a sense of what kind of loss he feels, a sense that you can only partially express in words. You think, 'He feels like *this*', with a kind of mental pointing to the emotions you imagine him to have. (It is somewhat like what happens when you imagine the exact colour you want to paint a wall, and then in the paint store you think that a sample is like *that*, the imagined colour.) So begin with imagining *this, here, I.*

Imagine Jo looking at the Eiffel Tower. You can begin to do this by thinking of the Eiffel Tower yourself, and thinking of looking at it, while thinking of yourself as Jo. That is in a minimal way thinking of Jo looking at the Eiffel Tower, though it is too vague to support any claims of accurately capturing what Jo's experience is like. But it does show how often we unobtrusively think of another person's perspective, just by thinking of the person seeing something, and assuming that they are looking from a point and in a direction. You get a more intimate imagination by thinking of Jo as being in a state that has those objects presented that way. You think of Jo as looking at the Eiffel Tower from the eastern edge of the Place du Trocadéro. You get a yet more intimate imagination, potentially more accurate and more in danger of being a misimagination, by adding more detail. You think of Jo as seeing the Eiffel Tower looming in the east as a symbol of hope. There is a progression of kinds of imagination here, from those that we can call transparent because all that is important is the particular objects of the imagined state, to those that we can call intimate because the detailed psychological workings of the state are also relevant.

Now suppose Jo is actually standing a little way from you, at the edge of the Place du Trocadéro, looking at the Eiffel Tower across the river to the east. You are wondering what exactly it looks like to Jo, so you mentally take up Jo's point of view. (This is something humans learn at an early age, and are from an alien point of view quite amazingly good at.) The early morning sun is blinding you, but you can imagine that from where Jo is standing it will be behind the tower. You have a vivid idea of the scene before Jo, with the rosy dawn light illuminating Paris, and the tower blotting out a swathe of it just where otherwise it would be too bright to look. Suddenly a bird flies from the lower observation deck straight towards Jo. You almost duck, because in your imagination it is coming straight at you. (Notice how this reaction is an updating of an imagined situation with information from what you actually observe.) Then you think 'but zooming right in, like that, it isn't coming *here*', and you imagine a last-minute twist of the bird that takes it from heading right at the focus of your imagination, where Jo is, to where you actually are. Your imagination has a double focus. You imagine the bird as coming right towards the imagined 'you', to the camera as it were, and also imagine that focal 'you' spot as not being here where you are. I think that this is the basis of the solution to the question of how we can imagine hatred without hating. My explanation of this has to show not just that this does provide a way of imagining in quarantine, but that the processes it appeals to are familiar and routine, not imaginative gymnastics. So I have to discuss perspectives and shifts of perspective in imagination.

We use our grasp of perspective to plan our actions and predict those of others. Suppose that I am imagining walking through a revolving door carrying a long parcel. I might imagine this in order to tell whether I could get through the door without crushing the parcel. Suppose that I imagine this by visualizing the door directly in front of me and then visualizing the scene looking straight ahead as my body and the parcel fit in and emerge. My imagination might then be accurate in that I represent the parcel emerging unscathed, but inaccurate in that I represent the event with a straight-ahead perspective while in fact when I later experience it the perspective is different: I turn with the door and look at the exit out of the corner of my right eye instead of straight ahead. It is as if the individual items of information were the same, but organized differently. So after I have later actually gone through the door with the parcel I might say, 'It wasn't the way I imagined it.'

In imagining yourself or someone else going through a revolving door with a parcel, or imagining someone seeing the Eiffel Tower to the east, you organize the information that you are relating the person to, in a way that is intended to match her organization of it. In particular, you have to match the way the person organizes information with a view to planning sequences of actions. When a person plans an action, she has to anticipate possible ways the action might develop. To do this she has to have at hand a lot of relevant information, much of which will not be used, and to anticipate how she may assimilate and react to information that might come in. One way, a typical and central human way, of managing this is to prepare a framework into which present and anticipated information can be fitted, and from which it can be quickly retrieved and related to other relevant information. A simple example is seeing space in terms of directions and distances to one's own location, even as one moves, providing a quick guide to bodily actions, reactions to things coming towards one, and paths of approach and escape. The result is like a coordinate system in geometry, with oneself at the origin, the central point.

Another example is understanding past and future in terms of stages in the lives of a few particular people, oneself in particular. These two data-organizing templates, spatial perspective and narrative structure, are often combined to give the typical human perspective on the world: a fabric of interweaving person-strands, each strand at each moment being the origin of a self-centred coordinate system. One strand in each person's perspective, her own life, glows with a special significance, providing each moment with an especially significant set of spatial relations.

There's a clear connection with imagination. When a person plans an action in terms of an information-organizing framework with an origin and coordinates, she is in effect centring her imagining of her performance on this origin. Now suppose that the action is a reaction to some aspect of the environment and that someone else is imagining it by pretending to react to the same situation: that is, arriving at a sequence of actions governed by an information-organizing framework attributed in imagination to the first person. That framework *centres* the second person's imagination of the first person, to use Peter Goldie's terminology, in terms of the first person's perspective. In talking of centred imagination, I am using spatial perspective as the clearest case, followed by narrative in the sense described. But it is a very general business with many forms. There is always a *this* reference, to *me, here, now, this thought, this act, this situation*, often several steps away ('me in the future, thinking a thought like this, somewhere way up north'). These are essential; spatial perspective is not part of centred imagination unless the focus of the perspective is the person being imagined.

Most of our imagination of people is centred, though the perspective can vary depending on the states being imagined and the imagining person's take on the imagined. They do not vary too much, though. For there are common themes to the variety of perspectives we have on our actions. Self-centred spatial representation and agent-centred narration are rarely absent. And the structures we use to organize our thinking even about very abstract matters have to respect the fixed limits of short-term memory, of speed of recall, and of ability to handle complex information. In fact, the main point of these structures is to allow us to manage these limitations. As a result, when one person imagines another, they usually attribute to that other person a perspective not too unlike the one that the other is actually using.

That does not mean that centred imagining is always an explicit, deliberate, or conscious business. Consider dances and conversations. When one person dances with another, in a traditional two-person dance, each tries to stay mentally half a step ahead of the other by imagining the other's dance-planning from the other's point of view, an imagining that forms part of their own dance-planning. This happens without much deliberation; indeed more than minimal deliberation would upset it. Similarly, when one person talks to another, she imagines the conversational direction of the other and the reactions the other will have to what she says. As with dancing, this happens more by learned instinct than by explicit planning. And as with dancing, the imagination is mutual: each is imagining the other and to some extent imagining the other's imagining of them. Human social life is a fabric of such shared imaginative projects, projects which could not even get off the ground were our imaginations of one another not by and large reasonably accurate.

Now that the pieces are in place, return to two-centred imagination. One person, Una, is imagining the emotions of another, Duo, towards a third, Tertia. Ignore questions of accuracy for now and suppose that Una is correct about Duo's state and situation. Duo's emotion is shaped on a particular perspective: for example, Duo feels that he is threatened by Tertia's future actions to him tomorrow. Una understands that Duo thinks of Tertia as 'that person who was outside my office yesterday'. So she imagines feeling threatened by 'the person who was outside "my" office yesterday, who might do something truly awful tomorrow'. But Una knows that it is not her office, so she imagines seeing Tertia loitering outside the office as if she herself were working there, while locating that office several doors down from her own office. One way of thinking of it is as 'right there' plus a mental pointing at another act of pointing, the first a pointing from Una's office to Duo's office, and the second a pointing from Duo's office to the spot outside it. Duo has a representation of running out and screaming at Tertia to go far away and never come back, and, intuiting this, Una has a representation of running out from the same office door and screaming, though she represents the point of departure of the running as here/there: Duo's office/her own. ('I know just how he feels, with the pressure he's under, like just screaming at poor harmless Tertia'; note how part of this description is 'inside' the representation and part of it is outside.)

Duo does not scream at Tertia, any more than Una does. (He just feels like screaming, she is just imagining feeling like screaming, and so imagining imagining screaming.) Similarly, when Una represents to herself Duo's angry thoughts, she does not draw actual conclusions from them, or use them as evidence. She feels the pressure in Duo's thinking to take seriously thoughts such as 'Tertia might suggest to head office that they audit my expenses.' She does not herself believe anything like this, though. (And Duo may not either; these are just things her anger pushes her in the direction of believing.) And she does not draw conclusions from it, such as the belief that Duo may be headed for audit trouble. Una is in fact unlikely to represent the exact thoughts that occur to Duo, neither the suspicions nor the fantasized intentions. What she reproduces is the *pressure* that produces these thoughts in Duo, as I discussed in part I. So she will represent thoughts and actions that are typical results of this pressure (probably with a bias towards thoughts and actions highlighted by her own concerns), which are not the same as those the pressure will produce in Duo. But she will not do any of these actions, and she won't adopt any of these beliefs. It's all imaginary.

(It seems to me that there is an exception to what I am saying here. Suppose that Una is imagining Duo's worry, and particularly focusing on awful things that Duo takes Tertia to be capable of. Then, although she does not have anything like Duo's pressure to believe that Tertia may, for example, suggest that Duo's expenses be audited, that possibility is now in her mind, as it would not otherwise have been. And if there is evidence for it, she is more likely to notice it. It's not a matter of a suspicious mood, as much as the fact, familiar to philosophers who write about knowledge, that once a possibility is mentioned then it is out in the open, harder to ignore.)

For the most part, though, when we imagine someone else's thoughts, we follow them in imagination where they lead, but do not arrive at that destination ourselves. It is as if we are tracing out the route on a map, but leaving our boots in the closet. It is not obvious how this happens. We are obviously capable of imagining a situation and noticing what our imagined inclinations to act are, without doing them. We can use this to predict the actions of others, as Robert Gordon and Alvin Goldman have argued. So, for example, you might be driving on a road when a deer leaps in front of a car ahead of you. You immediately ease off the accelerator, not because you are in any danger of hitting the deer, but because you know immediately that the other driver will slam on his brakes. On Gordon's picture of this, 'off-line simulation', in such situations you use your usual decision-making routines in a way that cuts them off from influencing action. They result not in your slamming your brakes but in your anticipating that the other driver will. But there is something much more general than this going on. It is not just decision-making that is cut off from action. Reasoning is cut off from belief; anger is cut off from muscular tension. When we imagine someone's state of mind, we imagine processes, but the results of these processes stay in imagination.

I have an alternative explanation of this. It is in two-centred imagining. Remember imagining a bird flying towards your companion from the Eiffel Tower, or the person planning a trip through a revolving door, or Uno–Duo–Tertia. The imagined thoughts and actions relate to *here* and *now*, but it isn't the here and now of the imaginer. It is like reading a historical novel set in Brazil in 1620: while reading, your thoughts focus on a certain place and time, but they are not the place and time that you occupy in your armchair in, say, Vancouver in 2013. So if you decide in imagination to run six metres from here, or that you think that this situation has got uncomfortable, your imagined run would put you six metres from the imagined *here*, and *this* imagined situation is more uncomfortable at the imagined *now* than it was earlier. The imagined *here*, *this*, and *now* are not where you are sitting and looking around at the time. They are disconnected from your actual situation, and to act or conclude you have to make an additional act of translating from the imagined perspective to the one you are centring your actions on.

If you are imagining the thoughts of a fictional person, then there just is no connection. In fact, you can be reading a story set in your house at the present, but it is not here and now but the here and now of the fiction. If you are imagining the thoughts of a real person whose situation you know something about, then there is a relation between the imagined foci and your actual ones, but that relation is information not available to imagination. In fact, the capacity to keep them separate is crucial to making imagination possible. So we do not need a special functional disconnection of decision-making from action; it is enough that imagination does not know where or when or who it is, even though *you* often know when is *now* and where is *here*. You do imagine imagined-by-you doing things from a basis of imagined-here and imagined-now, but that cannot make the limbs of actual-you move actually here and now.

Leakage is possible, as when you duck when a blow approaches someone else's head or when as in cognitive dissonance experiments you come to believe views you were defending for the sake of argument. But no special cognitive trick is necessary, other than that of thinking *here* twice. In fact, leakage suggests some empirical tests. If I am right, we should expect that when people act physically as a result of their imaginations, it is more often actions that do not depend on the actual location and identity of the person. As a result, we have a barrier, if a leaky one, between imagination and action. We can see how someone can imagine an emotion and be far from doing the actions that would follow it. This is not the whole story of imagining vile emotions without entering them. But it is an important part.

Misimagination

Vagueness is not error. Neither is incompleteness. When I say there are about a dozen animals in the field, I am telling the truth, even if someone might have given a more complete and precise report of three goats, two llamas, and six sheep. So if I imagine someone's anger and do in fact imagine fury, but miss the details of the retributions she is inclined to inflict, I am not misimagining her emotion, though I am imagining it incompletely. But I have got it wrong if I imagine anger when instead she is experiencing physical discomfort, benevolence, or despair. So what is it to imagine someone's experience rightly or wrongly? That is the topic of this section.

The vividness of our imagination of others and its centrality to our social life gives us a tendency to take our imagination of others as reality, to assume that people are as we imagine them to be. Thus if one person is in distress and another is sympathetically upset on their behalf, we tend to credit the second person with sympathy, for feeling the other person's pain. But the distress they imagine may be very different from the distress the person really feels – one may be the distress of loss and the other the distress of pain – so that instead of sympathy we have a worthy but blind empathy, as discussed below. Not only do we tend to assume that most of the time we get it right when we imagine a person's mind, we almost never reflect on the difference between getting it right and getting it wrong. Claims that we can understand other people by imagining their states of mind, and praise for fiction as expanding our capacities for imaginative understanding, are hollow if understanding a person does not mean getting something right about her. Or, to put the point differently, it has to be possible to misimagine why someone acted or what their experience was like.

It is not easy to say what it is to misimagine another person. It is easier to give a useful description of some other kinds of misimagination. If I am asked to imagine my aunt's face and I imagine instead my grandmother's face, I have misimagined. In general if the aim is to imagine a particular object or event, or the truth of a particular proposition, then you misimagine if you imagine something different. Of course this is only as clear as the idea of imagining something in the first place. But at any rate we can say that in these cases imagining brings with it the possibility of misimagining. A more subtle case is that of generic imagining, as when you are to imagine a green cube rotating about the line between two opposite vertices while slowly turning red. You might get it wrong by imagining something other than a cube, or a cube rotating about a different axis, or changing colour quickly rather than slowly.

Yet it is not completely obvious that there is an objective difference between accurate imagination and misimagination when one person imagines the mind of another. I am sure there is a difference, but it is important to appreciate that this is something that needs defence. When we imagine what it is to be a particular person at a particular moment, we are doing something very different from imagining that some proposition is true. We are experiencing and thinking, in a way that is aimed at another person's experiencing and thinking, and aims somehow to fit it. How?

Suppose you imagine being a refugee, forced to live somewhere where people speak a strange language, where the social rules are mysterious to you, and where the preparations you have made for earning your living are useless. In trying to imagine this, you imagine a situation and focus on certain features of it, causing you to experience various emotions, adopt various strategies, or form various beliefs. So you imagine emotions, strategies, and beliefs, and you imagine why the person might have them. You will inevitably get it wrong, in part. (Even if you have been a refugee yourself, your capacity to imagine the connections between the parts of your experience is likely to be inaccurate, so that you can make mistakes even about the subjective quality of what has happened to you, let alone its causal structure.) But if you want to have some sort of understanding of a refugee's life, you have no choice but to undertake some such imaginative exercise, knowing that larger or smaller parts of it will be wrong. You know this, but it is not easy to say what it is you know.

Sometimes what we do is much easier. But the problems in knowing what it is to do it right remain the same. If inside every person's head there was a clockwork mechanism, whose motions were that person's thoughts and produced that person's actions, and if when we imagine that person we imagine this mechanism and its operations, then accuracy would be a simple matter. You would imagine someone right if your imagination was of the clockwork motions that were actually responsible for that person's thoughts and actions. But it's nothing like that. A person's thoughts and actions are the result of processes in her brain, and broad general patterns of these processes are represented with varying degrees of inaccuracy by psychological theories and by the ideas of commonsense. When you imagine what is going on in a person, you rarely imagine the direct physical causes involved. What you do is to undergo states and experiences with some reference to the person, and somehow represent them as being why the person is as she is. So what can be right and wrong about this?

It is beginning almost to seem as if correct imagination of another person requires the impossible: that one become the other person. Even if we accept that we sometimes succeed, the barriers to success seem very daunting. And in fact there are systematic sources of error here. Social psychology in the last thirty years has produced ample evidence that our introspective sense of ourselves leads us to systematically false views about the causes of our own behaviour. Even when we are right about what we are doing and what we are thinking, we are often wrong about why, about the reasons that are making us act. So – projecting speculatively but not unreasonably from this – when we put ourselves imaginatively in the position of another person, we are likely to take as the causes of their actions what we would in the imagined situation take as the causes of ours. And these causes are likely to be systematically mistaken. If we are aware that this vivid and persuasive aspect of our experience may be deceptive, we may be more wary of other aspects.

But it is quite consistent with this scepticism that we often imagine someone's emotion and, while exaggerating or misunderstanding its role in their real psychology, imagine the emotion itself accurately, if incompletely. I will describe three accuracies that are components of successful imagination, each related to the others. Two warnings, however. First, imagining is more than knowing, in that we can know that someone is resentful, for example, without being able to imagine their resentment. We may know it because they tell us. But what this person's resentment is like, aimed at this target ('I really resent this party in my honour, where everyone is saying such nice things about me'), may be something we just do not grasp. And, second, imagining is less than knowing, too, in that we can imagine someone's emotion without having a real descriptive belief about it. Someone tells you how they feel about their parent, including describing actions they consider performing but do not, and fantasies which they do not really believe. Eventually you say, 'It's not anger, exactly, but something fiercer than resentment, and with a tinge of fear, and I have a sense of what it feels like, and what it might lead a person to do.' Both warnings turn on the difference between accurate imagining and accurate speaking.

The first accuracy in imagination is perspective. When a person's thoughts and actions are formed around a given set of reference points, relating ultimately to *me*, *here*, *now*, then someone imagining them accurately will relate them to imagined reference points. The perspectives involved in most emotions are variations on a few basic themes, and if we get the themes and variations right, then to that extent they are accurately imagined. Sometimes one perspective is embedded in another. It is not hard to make up stories in which Jack fears Jill will hope that James despairs that help is on the way, yet in understanding these stories one has to imagine multiply embedded perspectives. A similar complication comes from emotions to be discussed later, in which a person's attitude to a situation involves imagining another real or hypothetical person's attitude. Shame is the simplest example. There, too, imagining the perspective involves imagining a more complex structure.

Still, it is possible to get it wrong, even in simple cases. A person could plan an action in terms of spatial relations that do not connect with his own body's position and someone else could mistakenly imagine his actions through a conventional own-body-centred perspective. In this case the imagination would have missed an important part of the imagined person's actual thinking. So we can define a clear and significant aspect of accurate imagination as follows: one person's imagination of another's mind is perspectivally accurate to the extent that it represents the thinking of the other person in terms of a perspective like that which the other person is in fact using.

The second accuracy in imagination is thought. If a person's fear makes her think that the harmless little dachshund approaching her will eat her, then it is a mistake to represent it as a thought that the dachshund will frighten her child. If a person's fear leads to no beliefs, then it is a mistake to imagine beliefs as part of her fear. In particular, if fear leads the person to take seriously, in various ways, possibilities that she does not actually believe, then a very complete imagining of it will represent them too, not as beliefs but as conjectures or probabilities or possibilities. So if, though she does not think the dachshund will eat her, she wonders whether the dachshund would enjoy human flesh, or wonders if there is any evidence of man-eating dachshunds, it tells for the accuracy of an imagination that it represents these right, and against it that it gets them wrong. Including desires and intentions among thoughts, exactly the same goes for our person's desire to run away from the dachshund, her intention not to make any provoking gesture to it, and her thought that though she will not run away, it is very tempting to give in to the impulse to do it.

This does not mean that one has to imagine all the thoughts that an emotion leads to in order to imagine it accurately. Obviously, imagining many thoughts makes for a more vivid and interesting imagination, and one that is potentially more useful in anticipating the person's actions. And imagining thoughts that the person does not have, or relating the person to them in the wrong way, for example by describing conjecture as belief, makes for inaccuracy. But incompleteness is not error: one can imagine a very small part of someone's state of mind, and represent it well. Neither is generality error: one can imagine the thought that the dreaded dachsie is doing something harmful as an accurate representation of thoughts of specific harms.

The third accuracy in imagination is pressure. I described in part I how an emotion generates a pattern of tendencies to believe, intend, investigate, and ignore, and especially imagine, including motor imagery. I argued that the pressure of an emotion is a large part of what it feels like, of the affective side of emotion. Quite clearly, if one imagines the pressure of someone's emotion, represents to oneself the pattern of tendencies of different strengths to different kinds of thought and action, one is imagining something pretty fundamental about it.

Equally clearly, a full imagination complete with the targets of the pressure, the thoughts and intentions and images that the emotion presses towards, is almost never achieved. There are two ways to represent pressure accurately but incompletely. One is to consider only some of the targets, to imagine some of the impulses to action and belief that the emotion produces. The other is to imagine the pressure *without* its objects. Then one imagines just the urgency and rhythm of the pressure to believe, for example the frantic search for solutions to a crisis in panic-like fear – but without specifying which solutions are considered – or the slower and more sustained search in persistent nagging worry, again without specifying the possibilities whose danger is investigated. It is to imagine the music of the emotion alone, in its tempo, polyphony, and trajectory to resolution.

Usually when we imagine the pressure of an emotion, we combine both of these partial representations. For example, if we imagine someone who has a persistent unsure feeling about the contract he has just signed, we might imagine a couple of bad possibilities, specified in rather less detail than he is likely to go into, plus a sense of the general way in which his attempt to put his finger on what it is that does not seem right about the situation keeps coming back, while never resolving into a definite discovery or a specific intention.

Perspective, thought, pressure. It may be impossible to imagine any of them without imagining the others. But they are different dimensions of what it is to get it right about someone else, to imagine that person's emotion accurately. We do not aim for completeness in any of them. In fact that would normally be impossible. But we hope not to get them seriously wrong, for then the sense that we are imagining the actual emotion of the other person would be an illusion. That is a comforting thought, though. To the extent that we can delineate imagining that is wrong, we have some assurance that there is such a thing as imagining that is right.

Imagining invented characters: fiction and philosophy

When we read fiction, or watch a play or a film, we imagine what the characters are going through and why they are doing what they are represented as doing. In fact, in plays and films, and much prose fiction, there is very little explanation of why characters act as they do. In telling the story to a small child, we count on her imagining that the wolf disguises himself as grandma in order to deceive Little Red Riding Hood, and that her father (or whoever, depending on the version) kills the wolf in order to rescue her. We don't state these things explicitly because we don't need to. The occasions where we are left temporarily or permanently in doubt about the reasons for characters' actions, their general state of mind, and the kind of people that they are stand out as exceptional, and it takes a good deal of authorial skill to work them in in a way that the reader or spectator will accept.

Imagined fictional personalities cannot be an illusion in the sense of failing to match the real hidden motives and further actions of the characters. But they can be an invitation to illusion. This is because when we respond to fiction we react to the characters in many of the ways we do to real people, and so if a way of reacting makes sense with respect to a fiction, we tend to think that it makes sense with respect to real people. This can have two bad consequences. It can give us the impression that a certain kind of personality is possible, when in fact real humans cannot be that way. Or, alternatively, it can give us an impression that some kind of action is often caused by some kind of motive, or that some motive is a plausible cause of some kind of action, when in fact this is psychologically wrong. I am sure that both illusions are quite common, and should make us wary of claims that fiction educates us about human nature.

It is after all hardly a startling suggestion that *Crime and Punishment* is a misleading picture of a deranged murderer, just as *Lolita* is a misleading picture of a paedophile, and *The Silence of the Lambs* is a very misleading picture of two serial killers. And it is a familiar point that the characters in pornography give a dangerously misleading idea of what real people are like. Perhaps more surprising is the suggestion that many, perhaps most, fictional characters do not qualify for immigration into the actual world. (Just about everyone in Dickens! Or so I would argue. And this is not a criticism of Dickens, but one of his glories. Wonderfully believable impossible people: to real personalities as bel canto is to the sounds of speech.) An interesting example, close to some themes of this book, is Jonathan Littell's *The Kindly Ones* (*Les bienveillantes*), in which the personality of a monster is vivid and imaginable. The troubling question for the reader is: 'In having so

definite a grasp of this unreal person, am I being forced
to see some way I could be?'

In theory one could resist these effects, and keep one's
reactions to fiction and one's reactions to human beings
in separate compartments. To keep the two completely
separated would require superhuman control, though,
and might make it impossible to enjoy fiction. One
reason it is hard to separate the two is that we tend also
to think of real people as if they were fictional characters.
This is a consequence of the famous fundamental attribution error of social psychology: our well-documented
tendency to suppose that people's behaviour is more
constant than it is, that liars always lie and benevolent
people always help. It is our natural mode to populate
our social environment with characters with easily
grasped profiles of action which they rarely depart
from. As a result, if a work of fiction is to appeal to our
natural capacities to imagine the personalities of other
people, it can most easily do this by encouraging us to
think of them as more constant and definite than people
actually are.

So even when the personalities we imagine are like the
personalities we take real people to have, there is an element of illusion. Moreover, the demands of a plot will
often require an imagined personality that fits smoothly
into the array of personalities we attribute to our real
acquaintances but which wouldn't result from any combination of actual human psychological attributes.

(Is a fiction that encourages an imagination of a social
situation that is similar to the misleading imagination
we might have of an actual situation thereby realistic,
since it encourages reactions we could actually have,
or unrealistic, since it encourages a mischaracterization

of social reality? The question is like that raised by a picture which accurately captures the mistakes in understanding a scene that a person would naturally make, but represents the actual structure of the scene less well than a more complicated picture that represents the same scene in a more precise but less visually natural way.)

In a way, then, our social lives are works of fiction, which we live through a constant imaginative process which bears a very subtle relation to the psychological facts. Or so one can argue with some plausibility. The possibility should make us pause before being too confident in our imagination of other people, for it raises hard questions about the contrast between accurate imagining and misimagining of another person. It should also make us worry about a technique in moral philosophy and the more discursive parts of the philosophy of mind. Such as this book! The technique is to describe cases in which people do various things, and then to classify the people and their psychological states as one would real people. Thus a work on evil may put Hitler, Melville's John Claggart, and Milton's Satan on the same list – a historical person, a fictional one, and a being who is not real and also not human. A work on free action might classify the actions both of real people and of people in philosophical examples as voluntary or involuntary.

There is a real worry here, and an enormous question mark over a lot of what we say and think. We may be attributing emotions that do not exist. The danger of doing this is greatest, I feel, when moral ideals mix with our fictionalizing our lives. We speak of wonderful forgiveness for atrocity where all resentment has been put aside, and of condemnation of an act that has no negative feeling towards the actor ('hate the sin but not the sinner'). These may be real, but we should ask for more than confident assertions, just as we should ask for evidence when people say they feel at one with the universe or that they have intense love untainted by desire or identification. And in this book I tell many stories which end with a description of how the reader would feel in a given situation. But would you really? And does the description fit any real emotional state? What is clearer is that you can imagine being in the situations described in the examples, and that in your imagination you have an emotion which – from outside the imagining now – you describe in those words.

But there is an answer. I am most interested in the range of emotion, and how it is expanded by imagination. I do not take complex emotions, particularly moral approval and condemnation, at face value. I try to see how they can result from really basic emotions – anger, fear, disgust, hope – gathered and structured in terms of our ability to imagine from different points of view. This is not supposing much. A lot of it is underwritten by the observation in the previous section that if in imagining an emotion one gets its perspective right, then in that basic respect one is imagining it accurately. So we should remember the danger, and proceed.

Invisible everyday failures

We are rarely aware of the limits of our imaginative grasp of one another in everyday life, and of how often we do not manage to imagine at all. Sometimes imagination is too hard for us, sometimes we imagine badly and are content with inaccuracy, sometimes we do not bother, and sometimes we are unwilling. I think we hide this from ourselves. We overlook these gaps because we focus on things we do grasp, unless we are forced to retreat to more imaginative means. One factor is that in everyday interaction with others our purposes and roles are usually clear, so that we have a good idea why people are doing what they do, what their medium-scale aims are. That doesn't mean that we can predict in detail what they will do, for we do not know how they will choose to get to those aims. Once they have chosen their means, these often in retrospect seem obvious, so we ignore the fact that we couldn't have predicted them.

Suppose, for a banal example, that you have emailed a colleague a form to complete and get back to you. She may print it out and then fill it in by hand, and then bring it to you, or scan it and email you the scan. Or she may fill it out with her computer and send the file to you. There are pros and cons for all of these, but there is a catch with the last option. It is an annoyingly inflexible PDF form but needs her physical signature. You expect that if she sends you the form electronically you will later in the day have a chance to get her signature. But instead, she finds a clever way of inserting the signature electronically before she emails the completed form to you. 'Is this ok?' you ask. 'They do require a real signature.' 'But it's identical to a scanned signature,' she says with a wink. 'No one can tell how it was made, so don't be so suspicious.'

The means your colleague has taken is unexpected, but you know how to proceed, so you do not wonder about her motivation. You do not try to imagine what went through her mind, what emotions of rebellion and annoyance, leading to an imaginative solution to the problem. Life is too short: if you were to imagine her imagination, you would have set yourself the computer problem that she solved. So you content yourself with knowing what she has done and how it solves the problem. You forget the more challenging problem of why she did it this way.

Your interaction with your colleague was friendly throughout, and you were feeling sympathetic to her. So when she said, 'Damn, do they want it right away?' you felt a tinge of annoyance on her behalf, and when she grinned on producing the signed document, you shared her satisfaction. But it did not matter to you whether this was particularly accurate. You were just guessing at what you took to be annoyance and you had no idea whether at the end she was relieved to have completed the task or delighted at having put one over on the form-pushers. It didn't matter, and as long as things were going well, you didn't enquire too deeply into it.

The example was deliberately undramatic, because the point is how much we ignore in everyday life. But the colleague was being original in a way that might strike some people as uncomfortably thoughtful. Suppose that her device is not thorough enough and is discovered, getting her and you into trouble. Then you may ask, '*How* could you have handled it so dangerously?', and you may wonder whether her reaction was relief or delight at the end, although until a problem developed the question stayed hidden in the back of your mind.

Another example. A young man runs out of money while travelling in Central America and asks his mother in Canada for a loan. She sends him eight hundred dollars, and is surprised when he repays her six weeks later. He explains that as soon as he got the money he went straight to the casino and put the whole sum on one spin of the roulette wheel. It won, at twenty to one, so he can easily pay back the loan. She is horrified at the risk he took, and tries to imagine what drove him to it. She can easily see why he took the risk – to get the money and travel home without being in debt – but how he solved the problem this way is a mystery to her.

The mystery is not hidden in this example, because the mother needs a reaction to what has happened, and this is not produced by the mechanics of their regular interaction. (Well, it might be, if the son is like this regularly; then most likely the mother will cease to wonder.) It is an everyday case where someone has to attempt the kind of imaginative understanding that can be forced on us by an immoral act. Suppose the son had robbed a bank, defrauded a fellow traveller, or smuggled drugs in order to repay the debt. Then the mother would have had another motive for asking how he could have chosen that means to the unsurprising end, and the limits of her intuitive grasp of her own son would have been tested.

There is an interesting asymmetry between our reactions to admiration and frustration here. Suppose that someone you know solves a social problem with great ingenuity and tact (giving a loudmouthed incompetent a job that he can do without messing up everyone else's efforts, say, and presenting it as an honour). You admire this, and take it as a kind of divine gift. You don't usually look it in the mouth by asking how she managed to think of such a clever solution. Asking this out loud might seem ungrateful and grudging, and take the energy you need for applause.

Contrast this with the case in which someone bungles a simple task and causes more work for everyone else. (The colleague given the harmless job finds a way of using it to offend half your customers.) 'How on earth,' you scream, 'could he make a disaster even of this? Whatever could have been going through his mind?' Now you really do want to know why he took this disastrous course towards some unproblematic end, and you are inclined to go overboard with speculation. Partly because imagining motivation and emotion is hard, and partly because he is a bungler and you are not, your efforts may well fail. And it may happen that you think you have successfully imagined him, and taken appropriate steps to limit the disaster, until his next misstep reveals that you were wrong. Then you will be very well aware of your failure to get imaginatively into his head. The asymmetry is that admiration often blocks the desire to understand, while frustration or disapproval often prompts it, so that we are more aware of the difficulties in imagining uncooperative people.

One reason for the asymmetry may be that when the act is cooperative and successful, we can apply a basic strategy that Jane Heal has called 'cocognition': reproducing someone's thinking by thinking about it yourself, and assuming that all correct thinking follows the same path. When the act is hostile or unsuccessful, we often cannot locate the misstep by tackling the problem ourselves, so we are forced to begin with the harder problem of grasping what actually went through the person's mind. This helps us explain the resistance we feel to imagining awful motivation. In doing it we have to face the detail of the feelings and motives of the perpetrators, to grasp not just why the person did the act but also how they could have done it. We think that we do this for everyday cooperative cases, but really we do it much less often than we think. Usually we are content with the much simpler task of reproducing some chain of reasoning that leads to the right conclusion.

If you are a decent person, you resist imagining the motivation required to do awful things. Keeping these thoughts out of your mind, you make it hard to imagine the emotions of people who commit atrocities – if you try to do this by attention to the associated thoughts, that is. Your decency is then blinkering your grasp of others, not only in dramatic high-stakes cases but also when you need to know not why someone did something, what they were aiming at, but how they could do it, how they overcame emotional barriers to let these motives control their actions. When we do this we find that many ordinary actions are emotionally continuous with many atrocious ones. So we have a dilemma: we want to take imagination as easy, to ease everyday interaction, and we want to take it as difficult, to keep a distance between us and those we are appalled by.

The dilemma is a false one. No one ever imagines all the details of someone else's emotion (or understands all the details of their own). So we always have to choose what kind of imagination we want. There's the kind that works best for 'how' and ordinary cases, and there's the kind that works best for 'why' and drastic cases. They're often very different.

Imagining awful actions

Among the awful things that people do to one another, many are done for very clear motives: to gain money or power or satisfaction, out of spite or hatred or loyalty. Often we know perfectly well *why* someone committed an atrocity, but we are puzzled *how* they could do it: why that motive led to that act, or why the person acted on that motive rather than another. These are the cases that will concern me in this section, and particularly cases where someone acts out of hatred or fury. (I know that evil is done out of love, sometimes, even out of generosity or selflessness. That is a topic for another time.) My conclusion will be that part of our puzzlement is a kind of illusion. We raise the stakes for explanation of evil actions, wanting a greater imaginative grasp than we have of many ordinary actions which do not puzzle us. There is a basic connection with a theme of the previous section, since we demand a more complete imagination when we are less comfortable with the acts that resulted.

I shall make an assumption that not everyone will find

obvious. I assume that there is nothing motivationally distinctive about wrongdoing, that people do things they should not, and indeed awful things, from the same variety of motives and emotions that figure in all other actions. There is no special motive, such as the love of power, or sex, or contempt for others, that distinguishes wrong acts. (*Some* wrongdoers have particular and peculiar motivations, to be sure, but that is another matter.) I will not defend this assumption here, so if you doubt it you will not be impressed with some of what I am saying.

I want to survey some strategies we use to get an imaginative hold on actions that puzzle us because of their wrongness. As I suggested, the variety of ways an act can be wrong and the weakness of our everyday means for making sense of acts frustrates attempts to make the two line up. But consider some examples in which people do awful things, and we can intuitively get a sense of how they were able to. The first category is that of overcoming an inner barrier, and so I begin with a non-awful example of that.

B is pausing on the high board and will either dive into the pool below or back down the ladder and descend. A is watching and knows two things. He knows, first, that B is fearful, and in fact he knows how her knees shake and how the water seems far far below. He also knows, second, that B's fear is shaped around being in that position on the board, looking along and down, and imagining two possible futures (each in a different way unwanted). Now suppose that B after an inner struggle gets herself to run along the board and dive. While B is pausing, A has time to think about her situation and to use his knowledge of B and his own experience in situations like that to get a sense of B's fear. Perspective, thought, and pressure all come into this. A imagines the long way down as seen from up on the board, with some trajectories leading to possible belly-flops and others leading to impossible smashes on the poolside. In imagination he focuses on the sudden transition to the void, and the sensation of falling unsupported with nothing to hold on to, accelerating downward at a constant rate so that the further you fall the faster you are moving at impact. An image of Galileo's face crosses his mind. He does not think of the sense of control as one springs and the time one has to shape oneself to enter the water.

Then, to A's amazement, B runs lightly down the board, leaps, and does a perfect dive. A has to modify his imagination of B's state of mind to allow what he has just seen. He does not doubt the fear that he saw in her face and posture a moment earlier. He adds to it a fear of the humiliation of backing down the ladder, seeing it as a repulsive creature reaching out from behind her, and thinks of a leaping escape from it as an attack on the menacing void in front. Then, in imagination, running down the board becomes a choice of which enemy to confront in which, still in A's imagination, B can apply her training and her natural grace. Her fear of the height becomes a target that can be energetically, even cheerfully, attacked with the same movements that she has practised many times.

A is unlikely to use these words; what I am saying is a description of an imaginative sense of B's emotions that flashes through his awareness. And he may be wrong, however vivid his imagining is. He may be right, too. The perspective almost certainly applies. The thoughts, of diving mishaps and catastrophes, and of humiliation, are almost inevitable, though B will have far more thoughts related to fear and its finessing than A can summon. The pressure is the most delicate part. A represents first the uncovering of a list of hazards, then an alternating consideration of bad consequences from two sources, and then the summoning of resources to confront one of them while fleeing from the other. The most important feature of this sequence is the small number of thoughts it needs, and how vague they can be. A does not have to see all the hazards of either alternative in order to think of a vacillation between two classes of hazards, or to imagine another emotion, itself drawing on confidence, overcoming them. All A needs is a sense of the general pattern of pressure and what kinds of thoughts it tends towards. With this, he has a sense of what B's emotion feels like, and in a general way what actions it can lead to.

The diver, B, overcomes a mental barrier, and the result is admirable. But imagination can match emotion when the result is less wonderful. Sometimes the barrier is not fear but sympathy, disgust, or decency. It is this last that concerns me here. Suppose that instead of hesitating on a diving board, B is pausing before pulling the trigger of a gun pointed at the head of another person. Suppose that the other is her husband and after years of abuse she has finally been pushed to a point where, given an opportunity to express her rage and despair, and to avoid the beating that will otherwise soon follow, she is prepared to kill. Still she hesitates. She is not a violent person; she takes killing to be forbidden; and once she loved this man. But after a few seconds of indecision that feel like hours, she shoots. She will have overcome a deeply ingrained barrier against violence, and another against acts she has been raised to abhor.

This is a middle-level case, between the admirable and the despicable. Awful, but we can have some sympathy. (In fact, we might have more sympathy for B in this case than if she took the morally safer course, because of the burden she will now have to bear.) A's role can still be filled here: one can imagine B's situation both at the earlier hesitating stage and at the later stage when she passes the barrier and acts. And *one* way of imagining her emotions at both stages makes them very similar to the diving-board case. The pressure is similar: in both cases we have, to repeat the words I used of the first case, 'the uncovering of a list of hazards, then an alternating consideration of bad consequences from two sources, and then the summoning of resources to confront one of them while fleeing from the other'. The similarity is possible because we are leaving out the details of the thoughts, leaving just the pattern of pressure. (Suppose someone is writing an opera in which B hesitates and then shoots her abusive husband. The composer might be blocked at feeling the pattern of the quandary, the trappedness, and the escape, until remembering one day on a diving board, or even remembering watching someone else on a board, imagining what they might be going through.) The pressure gives a general dynamic template, to which different beliefs, aims, hazards, and possibilities may be attached to get an explanation, which may or may not be accurate of a particular person on a particular occasion.

Consider another case, with another kind of motive leading to a different awful act. A father leaves his child in the cab of his truck – in Alberta, in winter – while he goes off for drunken sex with his girlfriend, and when he returns the child has died of hypothermia. The mind boggles: we say, how could anyone do that? So consider an imaginatively parallel but morally contrasting action. S is a former nicotine addict who has weaned herself off cigarettes after a long and difficult struggle. One day, after she has been nicotine-free for six months, she is talking to a friend who is in despair over her stalled career and her failed marriage. The friend has also quit smoking but says that what she would find most comforting at the moment would be just a few puffs to calm her down while she talks. It is more important to be able to talk out one's troubles than to preserve nico-purity, S reasons, and so she dashes into a shop and gets a pack of cigarettes. They both puff, and the conversation is comforting, but they finish the packet, and a month later both of them are still smoking. Looking back, S sees the impulse to comfort her friend with a cigarette as prompted by the whisper of her buried addiction, and regrets it.

The story of S suggests a way of imagining the Alberta father. While the two women were happily puffing away, they could lose track of their resolve to quit. It was just nowhere in their consciousness, and the conversation was pleasant and comforting, just like the old days before the burden of renunciation was always present. If someone had disturbed them and pointed out that they had finished the whole pack, it would have been with an awkward lurch back to reality that they would have absorbed the fact. One can imagine – I think I can imagine – S finishing her last smoke and screaming, 'Christ, I left the kid in the car!'

My claim about the resemblance between the two

cases is very limited. After all, they are both fictional, and described very briefly. Real cases with real people would be richer and harder, and, being real, the awkward question of whether these were really the factors at play would be lurking. The claim is just that we can begin to imagine a set of feelings and their effects that fit the surface description of the Alberta father by focusing first on the feelings that we imaginatively attribute while reflecting on the smokers. The power of addictions to distract us and warp our preferences, the ease with which we fall back into familiar and comforting patterns of behaviour, and the subtle ways these two can interact, are hard to appreciate when baldly stated, but can be evoked with a suitable example, which we can then transfer to other cases. When the act or its results are not despicable, we allow ourselves to do this more readily, and the parallel may give us some tiny dose of insight into the awful cases.

Sympathy versus empathy

Many writers distinguish between sympathy and empathy, but every writer seems to be making a different distinction. There are three things to combine. There is emotional resonance: feeling what another person feels. There is emotional appropriateness: having a suitable reaction to another person's situation. And there is emotional identification with the other: having an emotion that makes you take their purposes to your heart and their troubles as your concern. All three are different.

The difference between the first two is shown by an example of Peter Goldie's. Two people are observing a scene of torture. (Goldie described them as watching *King Lear*, the scene where Gloucester's eyes are plucked out, bracketing the fact that it is fiction.) One experiences horror and the other terror. Horror is appropriate, for what you are seeing is horrifying. But it is terror that the victim is experiencing, so an emotion that includes it resonates to their experience. Of course one could have both – more about this later – but it would be possible to have just one, and in Goldie's terms the person who reacts with terror has empathy and the person who reacts with horror has sympathy.

But there is a third emotion that could fit the case: caring for the victim. Perhaps neither of the people cares for the victim, and while the first person, who finds the occasion horrible, is appalled, she does not take the plight of the victim as if it were hers. She has no impulse to help or to comfort. In that sense, a different sense, she does not sympathize, though her reaction has resonance and appropriateness. The same could be said of the second person, the one who imagines the terror of the victim. Perhaps she even enjoys it, in spite of being appalled. We might also say that she lacks empathy for the victim, and in fact when we are trying to capture this reaction we speak indifferently of sympathy or empathy.

No wonder the terminology is confusing. There are at least three concepts that we are trying to capture with two words. I won't insist on any particular distinction between sympathy and empathy, but I will speak of resonance, appropriateness, and identification, to label aspects of the emotion we can feel in the face of another person's situation, and our capacities to have these other-directed emotions. Several issues about them arise immediately.

The first concerns accuracy. We all have mixed feelings about the well-meaning friend who has great concern over something that is not really bothering us, while ignoring another source of great grief. Your useless spouse has left you, and while you are basically relieved you worry about how to break the news to your parents, who liked him or her more than you did. Ignorant sympathy then can be downright infuriating, though at other times one is grateful for any signs of solidarity, however ill informed. So resonance, as I am calling it, requires the resonating sympathetic person to be imagining what the person they are sympathizing with is *really* experiencing, not what they clumsily or sentimentally suppose is going on. But this links to hard questions about when one person is imagining what another person is really going through. And each person's experience is rich in detail, which no other person's imagining could catch completely. (There is indeed an adolescent attitude that rejects all sympathy on the grounds that the other has no good idea of what it is like for one.) So we must face up to the difference between imagining enough of another person's experience accurately enough really to be sympathizing, and emoting over something one just supposes.

And what is it to resonate to the other person's feeling? Suppose you are with someone who is making a big thing out of a triviality. He ordered decaf coffee, perhaps, and was brought regular. Now he is shaking with rage – before the caffeine has taken effect – and is on the edge of tears because the waiter was ignoring his wishes. You sympathize, in that you too would like to avoid caffeine after mid-day and you too find it annoying not to be listened to. But your reaction would be to shrug your shoulders, focus on something else, and leave a tiny tip. So you sympathize in one way: you share some of the annoyance. But not in another: you don't have anything like your friend's passion over the issue. You are likely to be annoyed at him as well as at the waiter. Suppose you are visiting another friend who has a very painful disease. You have some sense of what it is like and you are distressed that she is suffering so much. But you can't imagine the exact pain and her exact reaction to it, because there's a lot you don't know about her and because really vivid imagining of it would be unbearable. So you express sympathy while feeling a bit of a fake.

Then there is the question of the emotion with which the sympathetic imagination is, as I shall say, framed. In our favourite cases of sympathy the sympathizer's desire to help or to be felt to be on the side of the suffering person is central. But there are other cases. One child teasing another wants that other to be annoyed, even hurt, by what she is saying or doing. So she gets some pleasure from accurately imagining the other's distress, and if the other child conceals it she will be frustrated. So aggression and rivalry are the frame here.

You may think this is nothing like empathy. But note that in these 'unfriendly' cases one person is imagining the situation of another, perhaps very vividly. And it is perfectly possible to represent to yourself what someone is going through, including sharing their distress, without taking their side, wanting them not to suffer or to succeed in their project. For example, you are watching a boxing match and want boxer A to win (he's your cousin, and you've bet money on him even though you have mixed feelings about the sport). As he lands some good punches on boxer B, you wince and say, 'Ouch, can't take much more of this,' while at the same time seeing opportunities for A to follow up with a winning uppercut. Your reaction is complex and hard for you to express, but it does represent a person's suffering as suffering, and indeed with a vivid sense of its unpleasantness, while framing it with an opposition to the person's aims.

Then there is the frequent case of empathy with success or joy. We can see the continuity of these cases with standard sympathy or empathy when there is a trajectory from bad experiences to good. Suppose, for example, that you are rooting for an underdog sports team, perhaps the Toronto Maple Leafs. You care about them through a long history of failures and frustrations, suffering on their behalf with each new setback. Then there is an unexpected string of successes, leading to a great triumph (the Stanley cup?). Your feelings follow a parallel roller-coaster to the team's fortunes, from despair, desperate hope, and anxiety, to incredulous hope, worried anticipation, and finally exultation. At first you share the distress of the players in a way that we would have no problem describing as empathy or sympathy. And at the end you share their joy. We would not have a problem calling this final feeling empathy, and we probably would say 'sympathy' in the right context. And there is a clear continuity from one to the other, no definite point where the one begins and the other ends. They're fundamentally the same thing.

These three points can be summed up by saying that the components that we can see in situations where someone has empathy are found in other cases too, and in some of them it seems like a rather different emotion. In many central cases, empathy at its most typical, we have all the components. To see how they fit together in any particular case, we need to specify it in some detail. But they can come apart. And the appropriateness component can take different forms. Think of an observer understanding the plight of an intelligent innocent caught among critical intellectuals. He mispronounces a word ('Nietzsche', to rhyme with 'peachy', say) while making a sensible point; they raise their eyebrows knowingly and pretend to suppress giggles. He is furious and embarrassed, in no position to criticize them in return and realizing that the point he was making will be ignored. The observer realizes the embarrassment of the innocent, imagining how frustrating and annoying it is, and so empathetically feels his embarrassment and his frustration (*for* him). She also takes the situation as a shameful one and feels anger (*at* the intellectuals) and a protective feeling (*towards* him). She feels bad for him and feels bad about the situation. The embarrassment and the anger differ in that the embarrassment takes, as imagined, the innocent's point of view and the anger is from the observer's point of view. Sympathy can produce the same emotion twice, in some cases, once from each point of view. This can happen when one person feels for someone experiencing sadness over a loss. She feels sadness about the situation in which the other has the loss and feels sadness on behalf of the person who has had the loss. One emotion from her own point of view and one from that of the other, linked.

The conclusion is that our reactions in the empathy–sympathy area can vary, systematically, and which ones we aim for or expect will depend on our purposes and expectations. I shall say that an act of imagining another person is framed by an emotion when the emotion pressures the act of imagination into a particular shape, say by emphasizing resonance, appropriateness, or identification. For example, an emotion of friendly cooperation pushes us towards appropriateness, taking resonance for granted even though our sense of the other's experience may be inaccurate. Curiosity or aimless affection pushes us towards resonance, since it asks of us that we feel not something that will further some purpose but something matching the other person's emotion. And feeling helpful or consoling or protective pushes us to identification, since it prioritizes assistance and sharing. In a nutshell: we have to decide case by case where to place the focus of accuracy, what categories of emotions we want to find in ourselves matching those of the other person. We can't have it all, and we have to make some tradeoffs.

The tradeoff

We began with a question: how can you imagine hatred without hating? We now have some parts of an answer. The answer that has emerged is that you can have an imagined representation of hatred that has its characteristic pressures but applied to other objects, and you can have a representation of an emotion that focuses on many of its objects but differs in perspective. You can imagine something similar enough to give you the kind of intuitive hold that we use in most everyday social life. But we often want more than this. Because the emotion we are being asked to imagine is one that we distance ourselves from, we raise the stakes. We demand an imagination that is accurate on many fronts, and gives a rich sympathetic grasp of the other. But this is more than we manage in almost all cases of everyday understanding.

The double standards here do not only appear with emotion, imagination, or our understanding of other people. We find them also when we explain simple physical events. You are driving down a gravel road and a stone flies up and cracks the windscreen. You are annoyed but not surprised because you can easily understand how the car's momentum could cause a small stone to move fast enough to damage the glass. But there are many things that you do not understand: why that stone at that moment, or why a crack at that moment, of that shape in that position? Suppose that the crack is in just the right place to cause you not to see a stop sign, leading to an accident in which someone is killed. Did that accident have to happen, and what could you have done differently to have prevented it? You may feel you do not understand why the accident happened because you cannot answer these questions, because you cannot explain why this stone caused a crack in that position on this occasion. But you would not be frustrated at not having these answers if something awful had not happened. The tragedy is leading you to raise the stakes and shift the emphasis in what needs explanation.

In grasping another person's experience and motivation, just as in the stone case, we have to manage a tradeoff between completeness and accuracy. If we want to understand fine details, we have to relax the need to get everything right; if we want our imagination to resemble the other's in as many ways as possible, we have to renounce the ambition of comprehensiveness. The tradeoff is often fixed by the way we frame one emotion with another. Some examples. One person is afraid of a fierce-looking iguana. Another finds the situation amusing and ironical, since the first person has braved grizzly bears and maniacs with meat cleavers. So much is simple; she is amused that he is afraid. But her sense of his fear, the frame she puts around it, is her amusement. So in feeling his fear she selectively emphasizes those aspects of it that make her smile, though some of them make her recoil as well. It is like a sketch of a frightened man that accurately depicts that man's fear in an amusing way. Or consider someone's disappointed attitude to his own delight. He is sad that he is so pleased by a taste he thought he had outgrown. ('Can I tell anyone that I still like ABBA?') And – the framing aspect, his representation to himself of his delight (his attitude to his attitude to the music) – he focuses on those sides of his delight that disappoint him, contrasting with the mature tastes he wanted to have. His own delight feels rather sad to him. It is as if he holds a picture of himself being delighted, holding it by a frame whose shape, colours, and tinted glass direct the eye towards some and away from other elements of the scene in the picture itself.

It is important that imagination is usually for a purpose. The purpose usually comes with a framing emotion, a social emotion directed at the imagined person. The purpose behind the framing emotion gives its selection of details, which are the right details for the framed emotion, filtered through the framing one: the desire to run from the iguana, but highlighting the muscular posture that would face a bear; the free-association that the ABBA song provokes, but coupled with the kind of musical focus that is still aspired to. Remember the examples earlier where an imagined emotion is itself an emotion. In one of them you are faced with a stranger who is furious at you. You imagine his anger and incorporate your sense of it into your emotion. When you do this, you may frame it with fear, or curiosity, or with your own defensive anger. If the frame is fear or curiosity, you may feel the stranger's anger as part of your own emotion, without feeling angry yourself. You are picturing his anger via your fear or curiosity, and you are picturing it as anger, but through your own reaction. Your purpose, to protect yourself or to learn more about why the stranger is angry, determines which details of the anger you select and how you integrate them into your other feelings. So the emotion of preparing defences against just those things that an attacker might go for is an image of anger just as much as an experience of fear or apprehension. Shifts of object and shifts of perspective are closely related.

So there are three things one can do in imagining hatred. One can imagine hating something different, hating less violently perhaps and towards a more appropriate object. One can imagine something with the same rhythm and tensions as hatred, even if it is a quite different emotion. And one can imagine fearing or defending against the anger, in a way that traces out the objects and pressures of the moods itself. These are all related. In all of them one moves from emotions to mood-like and sentiment-like variants and then back to emotions again. It's delicate, and hard to do without misrepresenting the real person's real hatred. But everyday social life is made of these moves: we do them all the time.

All three methods require us to imagine situations that are different from the situation of the hating person we are imagining. That almost guarantees that the feelings we imagine will be at best a partial fit with the hatred we are aiming at. But then so it is in everyday life, where we ignore how partial a fit is given by empathetic harmony. One difference between the emotion we are trying to imagine and the situation we are using to imagine it is particularly important: moral quality. One case involved imagining a homicide by thinking of a person on a diving board. Another involved imagining fatal abusive negligence by thinking of a pair of ex-smokers. In each case the hold that I suggested the imagined case might have on its target exploited details of manner and motive and did not depend on any similarity of moral quality. If what we are trying to imagine is how someone could have done something, when it is reasonably clear why they did it, a comparison with something that is equally repellent is unlikely to work.

There is a connection between the mistaken demand for moral parity and the demand for more accuracy in imagining repellent actions than in imagining acceptable actions. When trying to imagine how someone could have performed an atrocity, we tend to choose another, perhaps lesser, repugnant act and try to use it as a model. Then we ask for a lot of detail and accuracy in imagining this and a high degree of similarity between the 'practice' situation and its target – more than we would if the target were unexceptional. (This is similar to the Knobe effect, where people are more likely to say that an action is intentional if it has bad results. In both cases we want more information about the psychology behind acts of which we disapprove, and when the act is awful, we are glad not to get it.) The result is that we think of horrible emotions and atrocious actions as unimaginable, when in fact we can imagine as much about them as we can *accurately* imagine much less horrible targets.

So this is how we imagine hatred without hating, imagine contempt without being contemptuous, for that matter imagine despair without despairing. We imagine a selection of details, enough to give the perspective and object of the emotion, to distinguish it from other emotions, to allow us to put ourselves in the other person's shoes, in the manner and extent that is appropriate. It is like a charming but accurate portrait of a disgusting person, or a schematic drawing of an atrocity. We can do it, but it may go against something in us to do it.

Part III
Memotions

The threat of irrelevance

Disapproval, admiration, pride, approval, blame, anger, disgust, disappointment, outrage, gratitude, contempt, respect, disdain, shame, remorse, revulsion. These are all emotions that can be important in moral life. Several of them are among the perspective-formed moral emotions that I will later call 'memotions'. But it isn't clear what this counts as moral life. Being nice to one another? Avoiding atrocities? Following rules that society sets for us? Obeying our consciences? If all these came to the same in the end, at any rate for human beings in societies like ours, then it would not matter too much which one we started from. But if they pull in different directions, then it is not clear what we are to count as moral behaviour. Consider the frequent eighteenth-century criticism of charity, that giving help to people in need usually encourages them to be 'idle'. (There are similar worries in our times about famine relief.) If the criticism were right, then there would be a tension between being kind and sensitive to the wants of others, on the one hand, and acting in a way that was beneficial for society in general, on the other hand. Or for a trivial example from contemporary life, think how we are annoyed by people who are too quickly familiar with us, especially younger strangers. We think they shouldn't do it, but at the same time we think that they have not broken any rules. So it is not obvious what the target for moral-toned hopes and fears is. The general point is that we want to know when to hope that someone is regretful (perhaps for a mistake) or contemptuous (perhaps towards a fake), and when to fear that they may be resentful (perhaps that one has told an inconvenient truth) or grateful (perhaps because someone has done their job more thoroughly than required). And we do not want these conclusions to depend just on what is conventionally or intuitively considered good or moral.

To focus the issue, consider theories that put certain emotions at the heart of morality. There is solid psychological evidence at work here, linking judgements of moral approval and especially disapproval to basic emotions of favour and disfavour, such as anger, contempt, disappointment, and disgust, and especially the latter. The psychologist Jonathan Haidt and the philosopher Jesse Prinz have pressed the point forcefully. The link is hard to resist when one thinks of the metaphors we use when disapproving of an action: 'that stinks', 'she did some disgusting things', 'it's a rotten situation'. Neuro-imaging data show that brain areas associated with anger and disgust become active when we judge that something is morally wrong. Moreover, as Prinz points out, moral issues prompt 'magical thinking': we will not even try on a jacket that was once owned by a mass murderer, or move next door to a major (but non-violent) criminal, just as many are reluctant to buy a house in which someone was murdered, or to drink from a cup that once held urine before being thoroughly steam-cleaned a dozen times.

The good news here is how deeply we care about what we consider right and wrong, how the judgements come from some deep heartfelt place, which makes us react to real wrongness as to something revolting or as an enemy to be attacked. (And we react to admirable action as to something shining and gorgeous, though the evidence here seems less clear-cut.) If these emotions had appropriate objects, their existence would itself be a wonderful fact, showing how essential doing right is to our conceptions of ourselves.

The worrying aspect is the nature of the underlying emotions, in particular the carelessness with which they choose their targets. We can get angry at the most inconsequential things and we can admire the most unimportant. Many things are disgusting but not wrong: eating ice-cream on spaghetti. And often we confuse our disgust at something with its being wrong. Many people would put someone who wiped his bottom with a clean white shirt in the same category as a habitual liar. The danger is that if morality were just a matter of heeding what disgusted, outraged, or enthused us, it might be heartfelt, but it could also be arbitrary, and potentially trivial or worse.

Philosophers who see emotion as central to morality have various ways of dealing with the problem. Jesse Prinz, for one, presents a complicated bootstrapping process whereby primitive notions of anger or disgust get tied to social rules which they enforce, and then become 'sentiments', with the content that an act is *morally* disgusting or infuriating. Prinz accepts the consequence that trivial or dreadful social rules can be the bases of such sentiments, but insists that the acts in question are wrong 'for' the people concerned. Shaun Nichols has a different solution. The final two chapters of his *Sentimental Rules*, 'The Genealogy of Morals' and 'Moral Progress', are concerned with the ways in which one set of moral principles replaces another, so that something closer to what we might take to be morality can replace something more primitive. Nichols concludes that one set of principles can have more 'cultural fitness' than another, when it appeals to basic powerful emotions that make them memorable. (This is an example of Dan Sperber's 'epidemiological' approach to the transmission of ideas.) Among the vivid principles are those which are motivated by empathy and the avoidance of harm.

There are deep and difficult issues here. But I think that the way they are posed closes off some important possibilities that I will be trying to open in much of the rest of the book. The narrowing happens when we try to make a direct connection between simple emotions such as disgust, and moral judgements such as that an act is wrong. To focus only on these connections ignores all the less basic emotions we can have that play a role in our moral lives. Shame is an obvious example, and it is significant that it does not have simple connections with beliefs about right and wrong. And more subtly, it restricts our thinking to consider the belief that an act is right or wrong as a simple judgement. For there are many different things we can be judging when we take something to be wrong (or right, or horrific, or . . .). Many of them are closely tied to complex moral emotions. For example, when we take an action to be morally admirable, we are obviously making some connection with the emotion of admiration: we are thinking that someone might admire it.

So my procedure will be to look closely at the moral emotions, seeing how imagination, particularly imagining points of view, is involved in them. The aim is to avoid counting as right for someone an action that thought and discussion would have cured them of (a danger for Prinz). Also to see how we can extract from popular prejudice principles that should count as serious evaluations (an aspiration for Nichols). I will be looking for ways in which there are advantages to feeling one emotion rather than another. For example, one might feel a gentle regret rather than the biting remorse people sometimes feel for minor misdeeds or events completely out of their control. Or one might feel amusement rather than outrage at naughty children, and severity rather than amusement at sexist jokes. These might be good for us, in that we might be generally better off, happier, and less inclined to regret.

Examples from smugness, controversial though they are, fit well with my themes. If smugness, priggery, and hypocrisy are part of the moral emotions package, then we can expect variations in them, depending on how the package is tuned. Surely, decent people do not have to be self-righteous. The upshot is that it matters *which* moral emotions we have. Some may make morality irrelevant or even perverse. It may seem perverse even to suggest that morality can be less than admirable. But think of it this way. Generosity, compassion, and resistance to injustice are qualities we should revere and encourage. They are also features of most packages of linked moral emotions. Does that give all the packages the same lustre? That depends on what else they contain.

Retracting emotions

You have a friend who sometimes really annoys you, but not always, and you can't see much of a pattern. One day she says something harmless which you interpret as an invasion of your privacy. (She repeats what you once told her, that, say, a few years ago you wrote an autobiographical novel, but never tried to publish it.) You tell her off, fiercely; your manner is tense and unyielding. The next day it all seems different, and you apologize, saying to her, 'I don't know why I got so angry.' But there's no taking back the anger; it happened.

Emotions and words are different. You told your friend she was overstepping the bounds of friendship, and the next day you can say, 'That was just wrong, false; nothing wrong with telling me what I once said.' There's no undoing the earlier act of assertion, but the content can be withdrawn, notably when you come to think it may not be true. In contrast, emotions are not true or false in any simple way, so there is no simple way of retracting them.

But there is something like retracting an emotion. In the case of your friend, you can feel regret about the way you felt the day before. And you can feel an emotion which we don't have a simple name for, in which you feel towards the object of the original emotion something that nullifies its effects. It is important to me to be able to describe these emotions of retraction, as they are linked to the difference between impulsive or instinctive and considered or experienced emotions. In this section I am just raising some intuitions about the phenomenon, which I will return to later. To get a sense of the ways in which an emotion can be retracted, and the emotions that can do the retracting, consider first two examples. To sympathize with the first you may have to put together a different story appropriate to your own personality in the way that fits my own misbehaving manner. You are riding in an elevator on a rainy day, carrying an umbrella that drips water on the shoes of an elegantly dressed woman. 'I'm sorry,' you say, 'I've just come in and it's pouring out there.' She just sniffs, sticks her nose in the air, and looks away. 'Well, madam,' you say, 'I withdraw my apology. I hope your shoes need complete repolishing.'

In this story you have withdrawn the gesture that your words made. But it could happen without any words, or indeed any communication. You drip water onto her shoes, though she does not notice, and you feel regret. Then she presses the 'shut' button to prevent the elevator waiting for a soaked mother and child rushing towards it. You now mentally undo your regretful feeling. You re-create the earlier moment in your imagination and you enjoy the offence to her elegance. Or you feel a different emotion which refers to that same past moment and mixes the feeling of regret into something very different.

In the second example you are walking in the woods after a campfire breakfast in which your friends were telling stories of bears. The sun is just rising and there is fog all around. You hear a noise behind you, turn around, and there is a large black shape motionless only ten feet away. You return to the tent, trembling, and tell your friends, 'I just saw a bear; it scared me to death!' When the day is brighter, several of you return to the spot and you are abashed to find that the large black shape is a tree stump. 'Still afraid of the bear?' your friends say, teasingly.

You realize you never were frightened by a bear, for there was no bear to frighten you. You retrospectively understand that no bear frightened you, though there was a stump that frightened you, and you were frightened as if by a bear. (You did not think of some bear, 'Yikes, he's right behind me!' though you did think, 'Yikes, there's a bear right behind me!') So you have taken the emotion back in this sense: at first you would have said, 'I'm afraid of a bear,' and later you would have said, 'I had a fright, because I thought there was a bear.'

What these two examples have in common is that there is a later attitude to an earlier emotion that neutralizes it, which has much the same effect as realizing that something you had thought is wrong. In the elevator case your later feeling is one of un-apologizing to the woman. As I first told the story, you un-apologized out loud, but the development of your attitude to her would have been the same if you had simply had the feelings that accompanied what you said. You transfer her from the category of people whose good opinion you care about to that of people you have some degree of antagonism towards. In the bear case you feel embarrassed about your earlier fear, and see it as the kind of fear a hasty and ridiculous person would have. (You are probably being too hard on yourself.) It is like being afraid of ghosts in the dark, or startling at moving shadows. In both the elevator and bear cases your later reaction is stronger than simply wishing that you had not had the emotion that you did. That would be true if having the emotion got you into trouble, or raised your blood pressure ('I wish I didn't get so angry at her, but she is so very annoying'). But in these cases of real retraction you are undercutting the basis for the earlier emotion by your later reaction. Your emotion about your earlier emotion shows it to be hollow, not what it had seemed, and protects you against returning to it.

One natural way of thinking of emotion-retraction is in terms of judgement. This treats emotions just like beliefs. You thought that your friend had abused your confidence, and then you changed your opinion; you thought that the woman in the elevator deserved an apology, and then you changed your opinion; you thought that the stump was a bear, and then you changed your opinion. But emotions can be retracted without change of opinion. Consider this hypochondriac case. You have a friend who complains a lot about a minor chronic condition. You find his complaining, and the way he manages to turn conversations round to his troubles, annoying, and you become pretty resentful of him. Then one day you watch him at an unguarded moment, and something about the way he holds himself and the tightness of the muscles on his face gives you a wave of sympathy for him. You might say that you had come to know that he was in real discomfort and often felt desperate, but you had always known that, and never felt it the same way. So when sympathy finally comes, you see your earlier irritation as petty and self-centred. You disavow it, and find that there is now a barrier both to feeling it again and to recapturing the feeling of your earlier emotion. (The barrier won't be insuperable. People *are* very irritating about their conditions.) There are many cases like this, and both the elevator and the bear cases can be fine-tuned so that opinions do not change.

When you retract an emotion, you come to feel another emotion that changes the nature of the original one for you. Then you no longer react with irritation to the hypochondriac, with fear to the stump, or with deference to the elevator passenger. If you put yourself imaginatively back into the situation, you have difficulty re-creating the emotions you have now retracted. (A special case is the prejudices of the past. When I try to remember what it was like to think in terms of some of the attitudes that were current when I was a teenager, I find that it is like trying to imagine an alien being. Things we have all come to feel since then make it very hard for me to revisit that territory.)

Now I can restate the point that ended the previous section. If we want to do justice to the ways in which we do and should interact with others, and plan our lives, we have to make our capacity for emotion central. But we want to centre on emotions that are susceptible to retraction, that can be undermined by other emotions we might form on more experience or more reflection. And we do not want to make the process of retraction just a quirk of replacing one feeling with another. The emotions that it is in our interest that people feel are ones that survive a full mature emotional education. We want to leave room for people to grow up.

Emotions with multiple points of view

We are interested in sophisticated moral emotions, in the hope that some of them are good ones to have and to encourage. We want to consider emotions that can be taken back, in the way I have been describing, so that a person can move beyond their original feeling. Given the discussion in parts I and II, the obvious place to look is among emotions that make sophisticated use of real and supposed points of view.

A clue that perspective has something to do with our question comes from the link between perspective and objectivity. Suppose that while you are so angry at your friend for reminding you what you once said, you ask yourself how someone else who knew the facts would react, preferably someone sensible and judicious. Quite likely you would think that such a person would not be as angry as you, and this would dampen your anger a bit. Instead of simply thinking that such a person would not be angry, you could react to the situation from the perspective of such a person. As a step towards this, you could imagine how they would feel, as vividly as you could, and, as I argued in part II, that would amount to having an emotion towards it. A calmer emotion would be some sort of retraction of your immediate anger. We do often appeal to how a wise neutral person would react, and we express this by speaking of some things as objectively infuriating or disgusting. 'Objective' here means, I think, not that it is some sort of physical fact, but that a person who saw the situation objectively – that is, not through one's own eyes – would react that way. A rough and vague idea, but one we get a lot of use from.

Emotions incorporating several points of view are certainly found among sophisticated attitudes to moral situations. Contrast three versions of condemnation, shame, and remorse. First consider very crude condemnation, thought of as anger towards someone because they have done something. Contrast this with an only slightly less crude shame, as a fearful sense of someone with social power who has seen you do something bad. (Your mother-in-law has discovered the vegetables rotting in the back of your refrigerator.) And now, thirdly, consider mature remorse, thought of as a haunting sense of how an act of yours would be seen unfavourably by a hypothetical person who embodies standards that you endorse. I will discuss the differences between such emotions in part IV. The important feature now is how we can combine simpler emotions into more complex ones by using real and imagined perspectives. So a person can be angry at herself. (For this she needs a sense of self, a first step towards imagining how another might see her.) Or she can be fearful that some particular person might be angry at her. Or she might be fearful that some unknown person would be angry at her, or that she might later be angry at her earlier self. Or she might be fearful that some particular or hypothetical person who knew certain things about her would be angry at her. This suggests three linked dimensions along which we can increase the complexity of an emotion. First there is the addition of an extra point of view. Second there is the emotion which is directed from this point of view. Third there is the status of the imagined occupant of this point of view: real, hypothetical, human, divine, or whatever. (Someone might fear that a mouse looking up from the floor would find her ridiculous, as Derrida felt the gaze of his cat. This is not a frequent enough emotion for us to have a name for it.) These can be combined in many ways.

One area in which these combine is in humour. Philosophers often compare moral sentiment to humour in order to make very general points about the objectivity of sentiment and judgement. These points could be made with other examples too, but I think that there is a reason why the example of humour keeps returning. There are deep analogies between humour and moral attitudes. Important disanalogies too. To begin, there are complex points of view. Without giving a definitive serious account of humour, which I have more sense than to try, we can see that the heart of a funny situation is often the discrepancy between two points of view. A proud and self-centred person slips and falls ridiculously on his bottom: there is his own view of himself and the one the audience suddenly gets. Or consider a philosophical joke, 'The optimist trusts that this is the best of all possible worlds – and the pessimist fears that he might just be right': the one intellectual perspective suddenly reverses itself into the other. And beneath all of these there is the fundamental duality of a pile of soon-to-putrefy flesh that thinks that it is the pinnacle of creation. ('How noble in Reason! how infinite in faculties! in form and moving how express and admirable! In action how like an Angel! in apprehension how like a god! the beauty of the world! the paragon of animals! and yet to me, what is this quintessence of dust?')

The resemblance continues when we see the comic possibilities of moral situations, often from a perverse or nasty point of view. The basic conflict of perspectives is between that of an aggressor and that of a victim: if I defraud you, I may think the situation is wonderful, as I can finally pay my gambling debts, but of course from your point of view it is anything but. We have delight and anger directed at the same situation. There is an additional amusing discord between the self-image of victims – say, rich tourists in elegant clothes – and their behaviour as bumbling fools who cannot protect themselves. To enjoy the humour one would have to be fairly cruel, though decent folk shouldn't be so sure that they are immune to it. (Think of the tourist-mugging scene in the 1996 film *Trainspotting*, which is undeniably funny, in a dark sort of way.) To see such situations as funny one has to have something like empathy; one has to be able to see from the victim's perspective, and then find the discrepancy with one's own amusing. So the chuckling assailant or con artist has something in common with the sensitive altruist, though the humour is spoiled by real imaginative empathy. (Some will say that when you appreciate the pain of the victims the humour disappears; my intuition is that it becomes a very different humour. It's certainly no longer a chuckle.) Even a non-awful person can see the discrepancy between her own attempts to act in a principled way and her failures actually to do good, or the discrepancy with all human attempts, and find a certain grim humour in it.

There is also a basic difference. When you find something funny, the two points of view are in parallel, and you shift or alternate between them. In approval, disapproval, pride, or shame the emotions are in series, one directed at the other. A moral emotion, as I shall use the term, is a complex emotion built out of two others, as suggested above. The first is an attitude to a real or imagined occupant of a point of view. Typical attitudes are trust, respect, love, awe, admiration, or fear. The second is an attitude *from* this point of view towards an act or pattern of action. Typical attitudes are being pleased or displeased, or, for that matter, praise or fury. These two are combined in imagination, just as one can imagine a scene in front of one as if it were seen from high in the sky. And in a similar way to how visual imagination complicated by an extra point of view is still visual imagination, the combination of two emotions via an extra point of view is an emotion. In part II I argued that imagined emotions are emotions, though not necessarily like the emotions they start from. (Imagined anger can be like fear.) And emotions compounded with imagined points of view are typically different from either of the components. If you are in awe of a leader who is angry that a child has scratched her bottom during a funeral, your attitude to the child's act may share the anger, but it may also involve concern for the child as target of the wrath, or amusement at the child's innocent breach of protocol. In any case, supposing your awe survives seeing what the leader directs his anger at, the result is a species of disapproval. It would be better, normatively better, if the bottom scratching had not occurred. Of course, moral disapproval is more likely to take the point of view of God, or Reason, or Society, or one's own long-term assessment. (And so one might try to determine which points of view qualify as bases for real moral disagreement. I'm not optimistic. For me, a basic question about moral objectivity – moral realism, as philosophers say – is whether there is a privileged point of view.) The idea here comes ultimately from Gabrielle Taylor's analysis of shame in her excellent *Pride, Shame, and Guilt,* which has worked on me much more deeply than I anticipated when I first read it and wrote a favourable but not enthusiastic review. (So this is an example of emotional and intellectual retraction.)

Why should you not trust someone who doesn't laugh? Because his moral judgements come entirely from rules, showing no capacity to hold two points of view in mind. And lacking the capacity to switch between perspectives, some aspects to friendship will not be possible, in particular the attitude in which you can see something from your friend's point of view, appreciate it as such, and still not take it seriously yourself. Why should you not trust someone who laughs too much? Because she always enjoys the conflict of points of view, and thinks that what is humorous must be laughable. The person you should trust most is the one who can laugh and weep at the same time.

The variety of moral emotions

Obviously, an enormous variety of emotions fit under my formula. I'll count them all as moral emotions. Some are reasonable fits for approval, disapproval, guilt, or pride. (I'll discuss cousins of these emotions – such as loathing to disapproval, shame to guilt, and self-respect to pride – in part IV.) And some are very different from any standard moral emotion. For example, you could have an emotion from the perspective of your revered great-aunt, of delight at her great-great-niece's struggling on through an awful concert. If your reverence for your great-aunt is really that, and she really had an encouraging attitude to such behaviour, then this does count as a kind of moral approval, though a marginal and eccentric one. A much more important fact, to my mind, is that moral emotions as I have just described can be absolutely horrible. Someone might find it disgusting that someone was nice to a handicapped child, violating the condemnation of them enshrined in her sacred book. (I hold back from real examples, for fear of giving irrelevant offence.) That is a form of moral disapproval, as I am using the term. Of course, we want the resources to say that it is mistaken moral disapproval, a topic I return to in the next section. Sometimes I will use the term 'memotions' to refer to the whole class of emotions with the structure I have been describing, especially when thinking of emotions that may not be part of our image of an ideal moral agent.

There is a long tradition of understanding moral emotions in terms of imagined points of view. The Greek philosopher Epicurus suggested that his followers imagine that he himself was keeping an eye on their actions, and the followers erected statues of him in many cities. (We don't know if people in those cities then behaved more virtuously.) In a contemporary experiment people put more money in an honesty box in a room with a photo of a pair of eyes on the wall. It would be relevant to the ideas of this book to investigate how much eliciting unconscious imagination of a point of view affects different moral emotions.

For an example of a possible and easily imagined but unusual moral emotion consider a person who is raised by parents who constantly debate questions of policy and conduct. Years later, when trying to clarify her attitude to situations, she sees these situations through the perspective of her parents' debate, continued in imagination. What would their attitude have been? So here the attitude to the imagined perspective is one of love and admiration (and perhaps impatience), but it is not an imagined person but a committee, a process. Its endorsement or disapprobation of an act or situation is one of our person's basic forms of approval and disapproval.

Different moral emotions can conflict, in that one can

have approval-like and disapproval-like attitudes to the same action. A good example is childish naughtiness. You are the parent of a high-spirited child who has engineered a prank on a narrow-minded, humourless teacher (she sits on a pin, or slips on a banana peel). You disapprove, in that the act is deliberately causing discomfort, and, adopting the point of view of those who maintain order, you are mildly annoyed. You also approve, in that it shows an irreverence that should be encouraged, and a sense of fun that you like. So from the point of view of those who want to raise interesting, free-spirited children, you are pleased. The attitudes you have to the two points of view – the ideal guardian of order, and the ideal child-raiser – may not be easy to compare. You may have respect for one and affection for the other. Do you on balance approve or disapprove? There may be no clear answer. A similar conflict occurs in the face of a pattern of behaviour that it is in everyone's interest to conform to but which is less advantageous than an alternative would be if only everyone would conform to it. Your neighbour refuses to put her garbage on the corner where everyone else does, and this is bad news because the garbage people have to stop twice and in the subsequent rush they make a mess that can attract bears. Your neighbour instead puts her garbage in another place, promising to build a bear-proof container if everyone else agrees to put their garbage there. So you have contradictory attitudes much as you do in the case of the naughty child. In this case the difference in attitude to the two general patterns of behaviour – putting garbage in the one place or the other – is more to the front: you have respect for one as a convenient and established way of getting the garbage picked up tidily and you have hope for the other as a possible way of bear-proofing the neighbourhood.

Horrible and conflicting emotions can be genuinely moral. But not any emotion involving the constituents of approval, disapproval, pride, or shame can count. Simple non-moral anger or encouragement or hope is just that, even when directed at something that might evoke moral concern. If you dislike people who can hide their feelings, just because your slippery cousin Merle was so good at it, that doesn't make it a moral disapproval of such people. Your enthusiasm for famine relief workers doesn't count as approval if it is based on admiration for their lack of commitment to their families. An important case for my purposes comes when there is a lack of endorsement of one's own attitude. Suppose you feel a visceral hostility to, say, cheerfully loud people having fun in the evening, and you sometimes say, 'That's really objectionable; they shouldn't act like that.' But you have come to think that your attitude is based on petty jealousy of others being happy, though you cannot stop feeling it. So you do not have respect for the point of view from which the hostility is directed. Then the emotion is not one of real disapproval, though you might have disapproving thoughts. Without the respected point of view it is not a moral emotion.

A more worrying case is empathy. Suppose you have an immediate emotion of horror at seeing someone assaulted, from simple innate fellow-feeling. Surely that should count as a moral disapproval. Given what I take to be the typical structure of empathy, it does. You see how the incident appears from the victim's point of view, and you have a positive attitude to that point of view. It is a somewhat marginal case, though, because you may not have a particularly respectful attitude to the victim's perspective. Or imagine that you are a child bullying a smaller child. The smaller child's distress suddenly becomes vivid to you, and something inside you is revolted at what you are doing. One might say that you have an attitude to your future or more reflective self, from which perspective there is a negative evaluation of the situation. But that is more to label the phenomenon than to explain it, and it would be valuable to have an explanation of the link between empathy and moral disapproval.

Here is a conjectural explanation. In my book *The Importance of Being Misunderstood* I posited a primitive decision-making procedure by which a person choosing what to do in a social situation first discovers what would be a socially desirable outcome and then forms an intention to do their part in this. Of course this intention can be over-ruled by considerations of the person's individual interest, but I argued that discovering the social solution is often much easier, and can mesh with basic processes of simulating the thoughts of others. There is an immediate connection with empathy and disapproval if we see that realizing that something is desirable from a social point of view is to see it as desired from that point of view. But then, if one is acting antisocially, one has a conflict, wanting something from one's own point of view and opposing it from the social one. There can thus be switches of perspective. The process is built deeply into us if the ability to see things cooperatively – thinking *we* as readily as *I* – is, as conjectured, a basic part of human sociality.

This conjecture would explain something that naïve accounts of empathy and primitive harm-avoidance

have difficulty with: the ease with which humans overcome any empathy they might have to bring misery
onto others. For empathy often fails with strangers, or
even familiar enemies. (Empathy fails even when there
is not hostility or disapproval.) And the mechanism I
have just described can come up with a social solution
only when there is a common social bond, either an
assumption of an 'us' or some shared task. Without it,
feeling someone's pain is as likely to result in amusement as in inhibition. Assume, then, that any natural
violence-inhibiting mechanism needs to be the output
of a social decision-making routine even in the presence
of an awareness of distress. And assume that there is no
social decision-making when there is no social bond.
Then empathy will generate disapproval only within an
in-group. Whether or not this is part of the explanation
of breakdowns of empathy, I take it to be a not very
controversial truth, albeit a sad one, about our species.

Moral emotions, in all their discord and variety, are
generated by hanging simple emotions towards people
and situations along branching points of view. The
point of view can vary. Consider this quotation from the
South Korean Buddhist thinker Pomnyun Sunim, 'While
we are turning our surplus rice into animal feed, North
Korean children are dying of hunger. What would our
ancestors say of this?' Pomnyun, as a Buddhist, does not
believe that the will of the ancestors determines what is
right. But evoking them is a way of providing a point of
view outside present concerns which cares impartially
for a range of people. (That's the thing about ancestors: they care about all their descendants.) Ancestral
gods can serve the same function, as can a transcendent
universal god. Some points of view will be easier to

conceive of than others. That of a particular imperious parent or leader is easy to apprehend, and if they project a definite personality, then what they approve of is graspable. The point of view of a cooperating group is, if I am right, something close to innate. These two perspectives combine in the point of view of impartial observers distant from the immediate situation. And in this direction we come eventually to a completely detached but rather inscrutable point of view valuing only humanity, justice, welfare.

Such an etiolated perspective can give little guidance without an idea of what, from its vantage, is hoped for or despised. This becomes philosophy: perhaps there are things that will be hoped for or abhorred from any such perspective. Perhaps there are reasons why some principles should be imported. A solution is to equip the perspective with principles or rules. Their origin is a conceptual problem. And that is my point. Fierce parents are easy to grasp, benevolent ancestors are just a little harder, and impersonal justice-seeking abstract-yet-motivating perspectives are harder yet. So it is not surprising that in the development of individuals and cultures, as more conceptual resources become available, so too do more refined perspectives on which to base moral emotions. We can move from attitudes based on respect or fear of an individual, to attitudes based on the reaction of society, to attitudes shaped on principles. This is the progression of Kohlberg's stages of moral development (in rough form; and I wouldn't want it to be more than rough, since the Kohlbergian picture is contested in detail). Note, though, that this is a progression in terms of what is available, what a person is capable of, not in terms of what emotions a person will in fact experience. And least of all is it a progression in terms of what is in the interest of the person or those around her. Sometimes a sophisticated emotion may be available, but it is bad news if that – considered disapproval, rather than outrage, say – is what you feel.

Emotional learning

Emotions involving points of view can reassure us that our reactions are not arbitrary or capricious, as discussed earlier. Or they can fail to do so and thus undermine them. (My example was sudden anger at a friend.) There are many variants on the process. You may try to imagine the situation from the perspective of a particular person, or a particular kind of person. Your culture may have given you a sense of a normal sensible person and you may find this point of view accessible. There may be a difference between the points of view that you can more easily enter into and those that are more effective in undermining your immediate emotion. (Finding that your twin remains calm may have a different effect than finding that an ideally rational and well-informed sage would remain calm.) There is usually a difference between the bare thought that someone of some kind would react to the situation in some way and the emotion of reacting that way yourself via the perspective of such a person. It is the latter that I am most interested in, as I am investigating emotions rather than thoughts. Finding that you can feel such an endorsing emotion as well as your original anger (or whatever) makes it a more solid, less quirky, reaction to you, but finding that you cannot do the imagining that it requires makes the anger something alien and passing, more like an accident of the weather than a position you identify with.

The perspective you see the situation from may be your own, typically from a later time. As you explode against your friend, something may make you imagine how it will seem the next day: not what you will then think of your outburst but how tomorrow's self would see the present situation. The contrast may be sobering, though it is a different emotion and it is possible to be directly furious and indirectly calm. Or the next day you may consider the outburst and you may imagine how it would have seemed if you had considered then the attitude you now have. Now you imagine imagining now then! If the result of that is something very unlike anger, you will have produced an emotion that retracts the earlier one.

I think this is the nearest we can come to retracting an emotion like anger. We can disconnect the episode from the stream of attitudes that are our socially presented self by knowing imaginatively that the emotion would not be felt from the point of view of an earlier self, and by feeling an opposed emotion from the later point of view. Then what seemed like the earlier expression of emotion becomes something like a misleading piece of emotion-suggesting behaviour, like momentary demonic possession or an attack of a psychoactive drug. ('I know I shouted at you for an hour and threw things and burned your letters in front of you, but I don't really hate you; that's just something that came over me.') This is like the frightening bear/tree stump analogy in that really it was not 'you' who had the emotion and really it was not the emotion it seemed to be, but a passing mood or blip. And it is like the retracted apology analogy in that there is a later emotion that undoes the work of the previous one. It exerts an opposing pressure.

With moral emotions, though, we can get even closer to the kind of retraction that is possible for beliefs. Suppose that during your anger at your friend you feel that she has done wrong, in the sense that you imagine an impartial person being as annoyed at her as you are. The next day, though, when you revisit the issue, your imagination of the impartial attitude is quite different, not annoyance at all. So later imagining of the earlier disapproval is blocked, not just because you no longer disapprove, but because a crucial component of that earlier emotion, the imagined reaction of the impartial observer, just isn't the way it would have to be. The similarity to the bear/tree stump case is now simpler: when you try to re-create the emotion, there's something missing. It is also like the elevator apology case in that you find that the judgement or opinion that the emotion needs has changed, since you no longer think that someone impartial would think that your friend was in the wrong.

The last issue, change of opinion, connects with an idea from part I. Emotions generate cognitive pressure, as I put it, on other states, on beliefs, desires, conjectures, inclinations, intentions, and all the other ways thoughts are organized. Beliefs are only part of the picture, and even when an emotional state leads to no changes in belief, there are likely to be changes in one's *dispositions* to believe. So when a person experiences an emotion there can be changes in many of her attitudes, and as a result some other emotion may then be harder or easier to enter into, because its own cognitive pressure may be blocked or facilitated. For example, if you become afraid that there may be a spider in your shoe, although you do not think that there is one there, it is then obviously harder to hope that there is a spider in your shoe, and easier to be panicked about a possible spider in your shoe, but more subtly also easier to fear that you may be subject to heart attacks and harder to fear that you will be ridiculed for being too relaxed.

The way emotions make other emotions more or less difficult is important because it allows a kind of learning, which can occur without believing or wanting anything different. This is especially true of moral emotions, given their reliance on the capacity to feel from a point of view other than one's own. These capacities are changed by practice. A good, though rather special, example is the case I described above, of someone who has internalized her parents' continuing debate over questions of what to do. Suppose that this person comes to disapprove of a certain policy, because she feels the parental discussion group turning against it. Then over the next weeks the issue gets debated further in her head, simulating the positions of her parents, and the consensus changes so that now the imagined debaters are fairly optimistic about it. This makes it much harder for her to disapprove of the policy, and in fact makes her almost hopeful about it. The disapproval has been retracted and blocked as a result of the development of her sentiments (and her imaginative simulation of a debate). Progress, without any change of belief.

(The example may seem fanciful, a very special case. But in fact I think many intellectuals' moral emotions work in a somewhat similar way. They – we – imagine an ongoing debate between well-informed people who have rather more faith in moral objectivity than they do: the debate is fair and intelligent but embodies an assumption that eventually it can decide what in fact is the best thing to do or the best policy to have. The debate can go on, in the thinker's head, for decades. Then individuals' sentiments about particular cases are shaped by their sense of the current state of the debate.)

This is true of any moral emotion: the imagined point of view in the structure of the emotion is a focus for later emotions with the same objects, which may retract, nullify, or block earlier ones. So moral emotions are likely objects of emotional learning. I suspect that these features are most prominent when the emotion involves imagining feeling from an abstract point of view – that of a person of a certain kind – rather than from that of a particular person. These more abstract emotions are more sophisticated and harder to acquire, though. So another aspect of emotional learning is moving from moral emotions based on imagination of the emotions of a particular person or group to those based on imagination of something less particular.

A related phenomenon is the way in which one primary emotion can supplant another in the formation of moral emotions. This is the point to be explicit about an unusual feature of my account. Some will think it is worryingly unusual. For me, approval and disapproval are families of emotions. There is no such thing as *the* emotion of feeling an act to be morally wrong, though there is the verbal thought that it is morally wrong.

Instead, there are many different emotions, each based on a positive attitude to a point of view from which a negative attitude is directed at the act. Call this the unbundling of disapproval into its components. Why should we unbundle approval and disapproval, in effect taking unstructured disapproval (no core emotions, no imagined point of view) to be one of those fictional emotions I described in part II? Here is an argument.

Suppose that there was such an emotion and that you at first felt it towards something. Then you would feel disapproval from your own point of view towards that object. Suppose that you came to feel that this earlier hostility was misplaced, but you couldn't stop feeling it. For example, you might realize that the disapproval was the result of an ethnic prejudice that you couldn't eradicate. You would cease to disapprove; you would still feel hostile, but your attitude to the point of view from which the hostility flows – your own – would no longer be positive, so the emotion would no longer be one of disapproval. But that means it never was that, if it was really unstructured. Retraction in the face of changes in one of the component attitudes is essential to approval and disapproval; without it they are just liking and disliking.

A child's disapprovals are made of anger and disgust. A sophisticated disapproval can be framed by annoyance, amusement, pessimism, or despair. Contrast the naïve reaction of a child to another child's bad behaviour such as singing during nap time. The disapproving child may, on behalf of the adult standards of conduct, scold the kid angrily, where an adult might, for the first dozen times, smile and intervene gently. Or think of a yokel's disgusted disapproval of an intentionally provocative clothing style (trousers halfway down the hips), contrasted with a simple amusement (which may or may not be appreciative).

The point is not just that the sophisticated sentiments make use of a greater variety of emotions. It is also that the replacement emotions have a tendency to block the former. If someone who feels that his moral authorities would be disgusted at the sight of two men holding hands is confronted with the suggestion that the authority might instead be amused ('Look, they're a new couple; they keep spilling their drinks because they have to touch one another'), then the replacement emotion will tend to occur instead of the primary one when there is occasion for it. I will argue in part IV that despair at the limitations of humanity, rather than fury, is sometimes a better basis for one's reaction to atrocity.

Smugness

There are vile memotions, such as contempt and some kinds of abhorrence. And there are merely soiled ones. Of these, I shall pay most attention to smugness, but there is a long list: priggery, self-righteousness, self-satisfaction, prissiness, sanctimoniousness, prudery, moral complacency, and others. A complex case is hypocrisy, which I discuss below. These are moral emotions in the basic sense of having the typical point-of-view-based structure, as I shall explain. They are also moral in that they are a standing danger for people who think of themselves as moral. If it is important to you that you think of yourself as a decent person, there are likely to be situations in which someone else will think of you as smug. Worse, there may well be situations in which this person is right. (Not that this is so very bad: better to live among smug people than among evil people, though smugness has some relation to evil-facilitation that we could well understand better.) So when acting on principle, one has to bear in mind the possibility that others will disapprove not just of one's actions but also of the role that one's moral emotions play in one's life. In this section I explore what they have in common and how they relate to more basic moral emotions. In part IV of this book I will try to establish some connections between smugness and fundamental moral emotions.

But is smugness an emotion? Yes and no. A person can certainly feel smug, but the label of smugness can also be applied to her, fairly or unfairly, as a description of her character which is based in large part on the emotions she feels. (Compare being guilty: a person can feel guilty – or feel guilt, as we more often say – but someone can also just *be* guilty, whatever they feel about it. There are times when a person feels hypocritical, but more often it is a quality that others apply to her.) So I shall talk about what it is to *be* smug, with attention to what this says about one's emotions.

When you are smug, you feel approval from some respected source, directed at your general character and actions. Three elements are required. The first is an attitude to others, comparing oneself advantageously to them. The second is an attitude to oneself, which takes one's present state to be satisfactory, not needing any change. Perhaps both elements are based on truth: the person may in fact be better than others around, and does not need to change to remain so. She takes it for granted that she is, though; she believes it on the surface of the evidence. So the third element of smugness is complacency about one's own value in respect to others. Its pressure is towards accepting evidence of adequacy or superiority, even grasping inadequate shreds of such evidence, and towards refraining from asking questions or following lines of thought that might undermine these conclusions. Putting these pieces together, we get a rough characterization: in feeling smug, a person imagines a respected point of view from which they are compared favourably to others as a person. The emotion may be based on a particular act, but the imagined approval is directed at the person as a whole. It would be harder to be smug if you were a survivor alone on a desert island, for lack of others to compare yourself with. And someone who admits to many crimes and faults cannot feel smug about one of her rare good deeds, for there is no approval of her as a person.

Though smugness is not admirable, it can be useful. A recovering alcoholic holding himself to his dry regime may compare himself to others who do not have to wrestle with the same demons, ignoring that they wrestle with others, and holding on to this smug image of his toughness may be a tool for staying away from the bottle. Many unadmirable emotions are useful in similar ways, for limited and fallible humans. Hatred of murderers is less admirable than the finely balanced horror, despair, and resignation that some may briefly achieve, but if that is not available it is better than admiration.

Smugness has self-respect on one side and hypocrisy on the other. Like self-respect it is a cousin of pride. When a person acts well, she is entitled to think that she will be approved of, from her own long-term point of view or that of some standard of value. And some form of this attitude to oneself seems to be a necessity of sane human life. Moreover, the thought that one has done well where others have not can be true and justified. But it can go wrong in many ways. It can be excessive, in particular in the comparison with others. One can judge others by different standards to those to which one holds oneself, disapproving or respecting depending on who it is. This is hypocrisy. Or one can gerrymander the standards, so that the things one does well count for a lot and the things others do well count for little. This is a kind of smugness-generating arrogance. Different imbalances in the criteria correspond to various more specific concepts. For example, if one pats one's own back for honesty and self-control and condemns others for lust and erotic display, one can be accused of priggery. If self-control, tidiness, and social niceties count for more than honesty and kindness, then prissiness is the label.

There is a particular kind of smugness which comes from moral self-reliance. Suppose that someone has firm values which they live by scrupulously, in a society in which different values are respected – the only vegetarian in town, or the only believer in rugged self-reliant individualism. Suppose that in interaction with others our person understands the reasons for their opinions, case by case, but ignores them. They will think she is smugly misguided, confident that her own values are better than the others'. The smugness lies more in the overconfidence than in the misguidedness.

Smugness will return in part IV. There are two connections with the themes of this part of the book. One is the fact that many moral emotions are less than admirable, some in subtle ways which ask for reflection in our emotional navigation. We need to refine our way carefully towards the ones that we want to colour our relations with one another.

The other connection is with the retraction and blocking of emotions. When someone says you *are* smug, and you take the charge seriously, you can come to *feel* your smugness. You become aware of what were previously largely unconscious feelings. You feel the fragility of the way you compare yourself to others, feeling both the comfort of it and the urge to make it more solid. But smugness is a criticism, so you absorb a point of view from which your comparisons are seen as wrong. You may not accept it, but you explore what truth there may be to it. This is an emotion in its own right, which we do not have a simple name for. It is focused on the thought, 'Perhaps someone could see me as smug, and perhaps this should change.' We might call it the emotion of feeling vulnerably smug, and evocations of it play a role in the way we get one another to change. 'Get off your high horse,' we say, 'stop being so superior.' If we can succeed in getting the other to feel vulnerably smug – or prissy, supercilious, self-righteous, or whatever – then we have insinuated an emotion that can block and subvert other emotions.

Part IV
Families of emotions

The ideas and the questions

Here is the main idea of this book and how this final part will develop it. We can have an enormous range of emotions, in part because our flexible imaginations allow us emotions structured around multiple points of view. So it is a real question which emotions are best for us, and when. And since emotions with multiple points of view are central to moral life, the question allows us to wonder which moral attitudes are harmful, perverse, or counterproductive. One way of making the question manageable is to consider families of moral emotions – one example consists of the much discussed cousins *regret, remorse, guilt, shame,* and *embarrassment* – and the ways in which we can slide into one of them when another would make more sense. I shall describe several such families and how their members differ from one another. I shall also argue for some degree of parallelism between different families. (So we can ask questions like: what member of the disapproval family is like embarrassment in the *regret* family?) These parallels have to be fairly rough, in part because there are usually several significant contrasts between any two emotions. But they do provide a way of imagining emotion concepts we could have and emotions we might learn to experience.

A more suitable emotion is an empty ideal if we cannot easily access it. A crucial question, then, is whether having the idea of a particular emotion – a description of it and how it works – makes the emotion more available. Is it easier to get into an emotion you have a concept of? (Does the ideology of romance make people fall in love more readily?) I think we can see reasons why, at any rate for the kinds of emotions we are concerned with, a conceptual grasp of the emotion provides routes into experiencing it. The idea is that we can choose from families of emotions which ones to encourage one another to feel, and which emotions, including emotions that express sincere moral attitudes, are obstacles to our lives. An informative and evocative account of this can give us a rough map of the maze that leads in and out of these states. In what follows I discuss families of emotions, better and worse in emotion, and how conceptualization can lead to possession.

Shame, regret, embarrassment, remorse

There are many resemblances between different emotions. Satisfaction and enthusiasm, love and hate, and C. S Lewis' 'No one ever told me that grief felt so like fear.' Some are similarities of feeling and some are similarities of the thinking or action that the emotion explains. I shall focus on resemblances that connect emotions that play a role in moral life, taken broadly. So, for example, I shall consider resemblances to shame and resemblances to disapproval. In these emotions imagination plays a large role, as does the play of different points of view. And with these emotions we can ask interesting and important questions along the lines of 'Could there be an emotion like this?', 'Why don't we have a simple name for this?', and, most importantly, 'When people feel this emotion, wouldn't it often make more sense for them to feel this other emotion?'

One large family includes shame, remorse, and guilt. Embarrassment and regret are outliers. Embarrassment is not central because it seems usually to be so much shallower in its target than shame or remorse. And 'regret' can be used to describe a wish rather than an emotion, a wish that one had not done something, or that something had not happened. It can also be used for a real emotion that fills a gap in the list of emotions directed at oneself in self-accusation. Bernard Williams wrote influentially of 'agent regret' as an emotion that we expect a decent person to be capable of. Other philosophers and psychologists have studied these emotions extensively, because of their importance in our lives and also because of their harmful potential, that of wrongly directed shame in particular.

Some contrasts between these retrospective emotions are now standard, especially concerning the differences between shame, on the one hand, and guilt or remorse, on the other. Shame focuses on the moral character of the person feeling an emotion, where, as Julien Deonna and his co-authors put it in *In Defense of Shame*, 'we apprehend a trait as an attribute of ourselves which we take to exemplify the polar opposite of a self-relevant value'. In other words, the person experiencing shame feels that she is inadequate in some way that is important, as revealed by some action. In guilt, by contrast, the focus is on the violation of some rule or norm and on some particular norm-violating act. One is ashamed of oneself for being or appearing some way in doing something, while one is guilt-ridden about an act which is wrong for some reason. (Of course, shame often involves an act too, and guilt feelings often also involve thinking of values one has betrayed.) Remorse is yet another thing; I'll get to that.

These are all moral emotions in the general sense of part III. They all embed one point of view in another. In shame one experiences the contempt that could be directed at one from an external or impartial point of view. One simple form is feeling the force of public dis-valuing, as when a politician is 'shamed' when his middle-aged sexual extravagances become public. But the social aspect is not essential. To expand an example from Deonna et al., a person looks coolly at the manuscript of a novel they have put so much heartfelt effort into, realizes that anyone not engaged in writing it would see it as terrible, and with a sense of shame burns it. Seeing from your point of view how you might appear from another point of view is, however, essential. If you simply realize that someone else has contempt for you, but in no way identify with that attitude, your emotion is towards that other person – annoyance, resentment, or indifference – rather than towards yourself. It is not shame.

The different ways of taking another point of view are shown in the contrast between laughing *with* and laughing *at*. You feel that people are laughing *with* you when you share with them an attitude of amusement at something you are doing. You feel that they are laughing *at* you when you see yourself through their eyes and ears as ridiculous. In this second case you are likely to feel embarrassed, which is similar to feeling shame. (Some languages, such as Spanish, have the same word for the two emotions.) Similarly, a brazen fraudulent banker, indifferent to the despair of those whose savings he has annihilated, may amuse himself at imagining their and the general public's horror at him. But if he was not so shameless he would feel this horror *through* their point of view and be horrified at himself.

Just as we can split embarrassment off from shame, we can split embarrassment itself into two, depending on whether the underlying attitude is derision–amusement or dismay–horror–disgust. They can be contrasted by elaborating a different example from Deonna et al., in two different ways. First, imagine a male driver in desperate need to relieve himself who pulls over to the side of what he takes to be a deserted country road, strides into the bushes, and urinates. Then he realizes that he is in fact facing a horrified Sunday-school picnic. Contrast this case with a variant in which a group of his college friends place a video camera near the only spot where he, coming from a beer-drinking session from which they have hurried him with no chance to visit the bathroom, will be forced to pull over. They then make a video of his increasingly desperate searches for a suitable place to relieve himself, and replay it to general hilarity or even post it on the web. In the first case the driver sees himself through the picnickers' eyes as horrible and disgusting. In the second case he sees himself through his friends' eyes as ridiculous and contemptible. (The picnickers are over-reacting, and the friends have a moronic sense of humour, but these matters don't concern us here.) In neither case does he need to see himself as having done wrong, in the sense of violating any principle that he takes as an important part of the person he wants to be. We can even add that it doesn't matter to him to respect innocent feelings, or not to amuse dolts. Still, he will feel embarrassed, exposed-horrified-embarrassed in the one case and ridiculous-embarrassed in the other.

The two embarrassments are different. In the picnic case he will feel grotesque, dirty, and threatening. In the beer buddies case he will feel absurd and laughable, a figure of fun. In both cases he will want to disappear; he will wish it was not happening: primal reactions of unwanted exposure. Still, we can separate one from the other, just as we can separate either from the sense of being seen to have betrayed an important value. They are very close emotions in that they are constructed out of similar components, but they are splittable, in that one consists in imagining horror and the other in imagining derision. They differ in ways that we will see repeatedly: different attitudes to points of view from which different attitudes are directed. With emotions in the shame–guilt–remorse family the object of the attitudes from the imagined point of view is oneself.

Shame-like versus regret-like

There is a fundamental contrast among retrospective emotions, between shame-like emotions and regret-like emotions. Shame, embarrassment, and guilt are unpleasant states to be in because of the sense of a critical point of view on you. In the crudest form it is as if someone is staring malevolently at you, from the present or from beyond time. Regret and remorse are different. With them the root unpleasantness is the unchangeability of the past. You have done something, you wish it had not happened, and there is no way to undo it. In a simple basic case of regret you make a bad decision, and either because you were not thinking carefully or because of the way things in fact turned out, there is an unwelcome consequence. Your act may not be a mistake, in the sense that you would do it again in similar circumstances. For example, you may have taken an acceptable risk, perhaps driving along a straight highway in broad daylight at a time of little traffic. But something horrible happens – a truck coming the other way crashes over the barrier and strikes your car, killing everyone but you. You then regret not yielding to the impulse to take a winding scenic route along the side of a mountain, rather than the highway. But you understand that that would have been a silly decision: you would have arrived late for an important meeting, and the chances of an accident were greater on the mountain road. Or a forest fire threatens your house and you gather your children into a car and rush to safety, abandoning the rare West Coast sculptures that it has taken you twenty years to collect. You regret leaving them behind, but there was no competition between them and the children.

Remorse is similarly focused on the past. (You can feel shame while doing something, but it is only once you have done it that you feel regret or remorse.) In a core case of remorse, you come to understand how much harm to some person or persons or cause you have done. And then the situation of the victim-in-the-past becomes vivid to you in a way that makes you squirm and search for impossible ways of making your harm not have happened. It is as if the empathy that you did not feel at the time, or which had no effect on you, is now operating to allow you to feel the pain and resentment of the other person. Or as if you can now hear the appeal of that other person through the gap of time: don't do this to me. So, put in terms of primal imagery, while shame-type emotions present a judging eye looking at you from the present, or from some place beyond time, remorse-type emotions present a voice calling to you from the past. With the first you cannot hide, and with the second you cannot plug your ears.

Examples can be very varied, and could be divided into many different types. To illustrate the difference between regret and remorse, contrast the case in which you leave behind your sculpture collection in the face of a fire with a case in which in your panic to get your children away from the fire you forget that you had promised to keep an eye on a neighbour in a wheelchair, who dies of smoke inhalation. You have failed an important duty and someone has paid a price, and the remorse you feel takes the form of imagining the neighbour calling to you to drive him away from the fire. (You are likely to feel this even if it would have been very hard to save both the neighbour and your children. Heroic action might have been needed. But you did not even consider the issue.) In this case, you were negligent rather than wrongly motivated. For a case of the latter that is easily imagined it is best not to make the motivation too evil. Here is a story from my own life. In my thirties I bought with inherited money a house that had a sitting tenant in the attic apartment, a retired woman on a small income who had lived there for years and regarded it as home. I wanted the attic for my own uses and so I told her that she had to leave. She moved at some inconvenience into a somewhat more expensive place. My plans for the house then changed and I let the apartment to a different tenant. As crimes go, this is not grave, but decades later I still have the occasional pang of remorse over this act of a self-centred young man asserting a property right in a way that was insensitive to the situation of an ageing person with limited opportunities. In my remorse I imagine my tenant giving me good reasons not to throw her out of her home, and I see myself ignoring these reasons and proceeding on my selfish impulses. The painfulness of the emotion is a combination of the impossibility of doing anything now to remedy things and the imagined distress and anger of the carelessly treated tenant. These are wrapped around one another: she appeals to me and berates me but I cannot respond.

Sometimes what cannot be fixed had to be broken. This is so in some cases discussed by Bernard Williams. In these cases a person has a choice in which both options were unappetizing, takes one, and feels remorse or a particularly pointed form of regret. Two of you are walking in the woods and you come across a hiker who has fallen over a cliff and broken his leg. You are trained in first aid, so you send your companion on to fetch help while you stay to make an emergency splint and to keep the hiker comfortable until a stretcher team or a helicopter arrives. There is a cost to you, since by staying there you miss your chance to get to your mother's funeral, at which long-simmering family tensions might be resolved. You could instead have instructed your companion in the procedures and have rushed ahead to summon help and get to the funeral. You feel awful about missing the funeral even though you think your choice was the right one. You keep rethinking the situation, trying to find ways in which the hiker could have had the benefit of your skills while you got out of the woods in the next hour. But you never find a solution. Williams has persuaded most philosophers that there are many such situations, and that we want a decent person to feel regret or remorse in them. These include situations in which both options open to you have equally unacceptable features, so whatever you do is equally wrong. (You have promised to pay your friend's medical school tuition, but you need the money to pay your sister's way through a rehab clinic for her heroin addiction. Now whatever you do there will be bad consequences.) Then since neither option is *the* best one, you can flip a coin, choose one, and go on your way whistling, right? No, of course not: you may have to decide arbitrarily, but the price a decent person pays is to feel remorse whichever way they decide.

Williams describes these emotions as a kind of regret, 'agent regret', to distinguish it from the regret that does not focus on one's own actions (as when one regrets that Woodrow Wilson failed to get the US into the League of Nations). He might have called it a kind of remorse. There is a wisdom, though, in choosing a potentially more general term. For there are many situations in which although it is clear that things have turned out badly, it is not clear what responsibility one bears. For example, a colleague comes to you with what you take to be an unreasonable request, and you refuse it in very definite terms. The colleague goes away in a ferocious temper and half an hour later is involved in a car accident in which someone is seriously hurt. You think that if you had refused him more tactfully, knowing that he was a volatile personality, he might have driven more carefully and the accident might not have occurred. So you regret being so uncompromising and blunt. But how much should you blame yourself, how much should you take the victim of the accident to be appealing to you to have acted differently? Questions of blame and responsibility are notoriously difficult to resolve. Not only are the relevant causal facts usually hard to settle, but the concepts themselves are intrinsically unclear. So while 'Whose fault is it?' is often a pointless question, 'What should we now do, and what should we now feel?' very often is not.

What Williams calls regret is a large class of backward-looking emotions. It is good to have this wide concept, for the reasons I have just mentioned. It is also good to be able to distinguish remorse from regret, and within each to distinguish different ways in which the past can appeal critically to the present. These are not all the backward-looking emotions, though. They are the ones built around the image of a past victim who appeals to a present agent. That is different from shame and guilt, built around the image of a present or timeless judge who sees the fault in what the agent does.

Ghosts

Remorse usually has a haunting quality. In a model case someone has been harmed, the harm is irreparable, and you feel an appeal from the harmed person, which will not leave you alone. If it is a model case of remorse, you have done wrong in causing the harm. But we can be haunted by harms that we were not wrong to cause, for example by injuries to someone in a sporting contest. The haunting thought may then be whether one did wrong, and in spite of good reasons to dismiss it, it may not go away. Or we might be haunted by the memory of acts where no one was hurt but our behaviour appeared shameful or embarrassing. Alternatively, someone can feel remorse for one of her crimes, but only on occasions when they are brought to mind, when it is a real and biting, though somehow shallow, remorse. I shall assume that remorse is more frequently linked to the haunting phenomenon than other retrospective memotions are, though they too can be linked to it. ('Remorse' is 'biting again', the middle English 'agenbite of inwit', best known from Joyce's use of the phrase in *Ulysses*.)

Moreover, completely different emotions can also haunt us. Disgust can return uninvited, a wistful memory of a perfect day can become a frequent backdrop to one's life. There are many kinds of ghosts.

I take it that at the heart of the haunting in remorse is the urge to rethink. You have done something with bad consequences and the question of how you could have acted differently keeps recurring. Could you have paid more attention, or prepared differently, or controlled your impulses more? Why did you act this way, think this way, yield to this desire? This may be a heavy burden on your life, and it may be unneeded or out of proportion. But the tendency to be haunted by mistakes and misdeeds serves a purpose. Similar situations may recur, and by rethinking you may make yourself handle them better. Long-term changes in character, as well as improved strategies for recurring issues, may be expected. You may grow.

When you are haunted by remorse, it is your conscience that is bothering you. We also speak of someone being conscientious when they are careful with their responsibilities. The two similar words refer to connected processes. When you have a bad conscience, you rethink what you should have done, and when you are conscientious, you attend to what you are doing in terms of what went wrong in the past (and how you will feel if this too goes wrong, though this is not so important from my point of view). In the case of conscientiousness it is as if the gaze of complaint from the past is now directed at your present activities. 'You hurt me then; now let's see what you're up to now.' Or, the other way round, the mistake-catching oversight one has over one's present conscientious activities is applied also to past actions, and finds much to criticize. So there is a connection between the capacity for remorse and the capacity for responsible conscientious action. They are loose connections, but connections all the same. A culture that encourages one is likely to encourage the other.

It is usually unpleasant to be haunted, and those who have nothing to haunt them can bask in their lack of ghosts. Of course, we all have some past conduct that we could well reconsider, so the feeling that there are no skeletons in one's closet is a kind of smugness. In fact, it is central to smugness, I think, and gives a deep connection between smugness and remorse. They are opposites – the smug person does not see why remorse might touch her – but built on the same frame. One motive for self-deceptive smugness can be an awareness of how unpleasant remorse would be. So here a crudity about remorse, thinking that the only kind is breast-beating hair-tearing agony, will reinforce a crude and dogmatic whited sepulchre of smug conscience. And conversely, a conviction that there is some routine and easy way to rethink one's misdeeds – one simply looks at them with a clear judgement and sees what is right and wrong about what one has done, admits it, and gets it over with – is at once a kind of smugness and the shallowest possible remorse. (See 'The smug family' below for more on kinds of smugness.)

We have here a fundamental way in which a self-consciously moral person can fall into smugness. Suppose that they subscribe to a set of rules for right conduct, and they know that they have followed them, while others have not. Then they feel justified in condemning these others, who should feel remorse. They feel no remorse themselves, for they have done nothing wrong. Their moral security is based on the confidence in knowing where the line between right and wrong is, and knowing that they are on the right side of it. Contrast this with someone whose reactions to hard cases are based on imagination, empathy, and improvisation – a riskier attitude, though we need it when, as often, the official rules are blind or unjust or crush individuals in the cogs of their approximations. (And as I say in the final section, part of what we can well imagine is exactly *how* others' moral emotions are structured, rather than thinking that if they do not parallel ours they are not really shame or admiration.)

Almost any hard moral problem will do as an illustration: conflicts between obligations to those near to one and to humanity at large, conflicts between one's own requirements and those of others, conflicts between the more certain short term and the less certain long term. There are some who think that there are best rules waiting to be discovered (or already known); there are some who think that there are ideal outcomes to which our bumbling efforts at imagination and empathy approximate; there is at least one who thinks that there is no single fixed target, but human life goes best if we are as imaginative, empathetic, and ingenious as we can be. Whichever of these is right, it remains that when you look back at how you were torn between, say, the expectation that you would support your child through medical school and your cousin's sudden need to pay for a life-saving operation, a little more thought will produce dozens of alternatives that never occurred to you, and which might have turned out better. And if in fact the situation turned out very short of well, then you are going to be haunted by what might have been.

Someone who in similar circumstances did similar things with similar results, but who is confident that she did the right thing, will not be haunted. Her authorities look down on her and smile approvingly, though they are saddened by some of the consequences. She can smile on her past as her authorities smile on her. I will think she is smug, smug from lack of imagination.

Looking backward and looking inward

Different as emotions like remorse are from emotions like shame, they are all moral emotions in the very general sense described in part III. They are, that is, if we exclude the cases when we use the emotion words as metaphors for quite different states, as when we say we are embarrassed when we mean we have no money, or when we say we regret something, meaning just that we wish it had not happened. But the core regret-like and shame-like emotions are all compounded out of several simpler emotions joined through an imagined point of view. In guilt and shame one feels oneself to be the object of an aggressive emotion – derision, distaste, anger – from the point of view of someone towards whom one has a respectful emotion – awe, affection, subservience. In regret and remorse one feels oneself to be the object of an emotion of appeal – protest, complaint, recrimination – by someone affected by a past action for whom one has an emotion of concern – pity, commiseration, sympathy. The lists of component emotions can be extended, and we can get many variant emotions by filling the blanks in various ways.

These are what *I* take to be the core combinations for emotions of these types. Others may focus more on some features than on others, for there are a number of striking contrasts between any two of these emotions. We often use words for retrospective emotions very loosely, so that one could substitute one for another without much loss of meaning. (If someone says they feel guilty about parking in a disabled spot, and you ask whether they really mean that they feel shame, you are likely to be met with puzzled annoyance.) We also sometimes deliberately contrast emotion words: we say that what we felt was not shame but just embarrassment, or that someone is burdening herself with guilt when regret would be more appropriate. When we do this, we tend, I suspect, to focus on different contrasts on different occasions, depending on what is important then. Remorse has a greater emphasis on past-ness, also on there being an injured victim, and also on the biting recurrent self-punishing aspect, so on any particular occasion the point of stressing that it is remorse that someone feels may be any one of these. Similarly, guilt has an emphasis on social rules, and on judgements of right and wrong, and shame has an emphasis on exposure and betrayal of some value. But which of these dominates will vary.

There are more complicated moral emotions. In particular there are emotions involving a triple point of view. The most natural one is a remorse-like emotion in which one feels judged from an external point of view on the basis of how one responds to an appeal from a person injured in the past. In this there would be a respect-like emotion to a point of view which has a critical emotion towards one's reaction to an imagined appeal from a past point of view for which one has a sympathetic emotion. This might be what one felt if one was concerned about how untroubled one's conscience was. ('You complacent bastard', something in you says to yourself. The remorse-like emotion is a regret at your smugness!) In a suitable context this might be what was evoked by 'remorse'. Some complex emotions seem not to be possible, or at any rate to be going against the grain. For example, the emotion of imagining a respected past point of view judging how one responds to an appeal from someone one is injuring in the present: that is a perfectly conceivable emotion, but it does not sound like part of the human repertoire. One constraint may be that a past point of view must be that of a particular person. We can hope for psychological understanding of what such constraints are and why they exist.

The structure of points of view combines emotions of respect, emotions of condemnation, and emotions of appeal: all very general classes of emotions. The gaps can be occupied by different, more specific emotions. Sometimes we have names for the results of doing this. Embarrassment, for example, differs from shame partly in that the imagined attitude of the external point of view is derision rather than condemnation. (And the attitude *to* that point of view is less one of respect and more one of fear.) Often, though, we do not have a standard terminology for making the distinction. Think of the two kinds of shame in one of which one imagines anger directed at one for one's behaviour, while in the other it is contempt. There could be different words for these. The first is what one would most likely feel if one was caught sneaking through a window into someone's house, and the second is what one would most likely feel if one was caught looking up the answers to an elementary geography quiz ('Which of these are countries and which are cities . . .?'). But we have no tidy labels for them.

One reason we are short of labels is that we fill the blank with 'disapproval': shame is when you imagine someone disapproving of you. But this word itself can mean many things: even mainline moral disapproval can vary from abhorrence to distaste, and along a different dimension we react with a different emotional tone to crimes of violence and crimes of dishonesty. So if shame is someone disapproving of you and disapproval is imagining an authoritative dislike, then shame is a three-perspective emotion: imagining a point of view from which a point of view is imagined from which one is disliked. This isn't impossible: a person, Amos, can imagine how his deceased mother Beatrice would take God to be disgusted by his actions. But you can see how the possibilities multiply. (You can imagine someone from an advanced but rather distant civilization who understood contempt, abhorrence, and distaste, understood shame and guilt, understood compounds of basic emotions from various points of view, but was puzzled by moral disapproval. What exactly are we on about?)

There are gaps, retrospective emotions we can describe, and evoke with cases, but have no simple words for. Suppose that you feel an imagined fair criticism about your treatment of someone for whom you had and have no sympathy at all (a slimy whiner whom you squashed verbally with a well-placed witticism, say, when you should have been the neutral chair of a committee). That is generally remorse-like, rather like embarrassment in its lack of bite, but not exactly either. We would probably say 'regret', and then add some detail. Or think of deadly serious embarrassment. There are embarrassments that haunt a person for life, or lead to suicide. (In Aubrey's *Brief Lives* there is the story of an Elizabethan courtier who broke wind at court, and in his mortification sailed around the world – no trivial exploit in those days. On his return the Queen greeted him with 'We have forgot the fart.') The internet raises new possibilities here: a hidden camera could record images of you masturbating or revealing abysmal ignorance of some basic topic, which would be seen by millions and preserved for future ages. This would be lumped with shame in some languages, but not in English, assuming that you did not think what you did was wrong. You are not ashamed of what you did, but hate the fact that all these people know about it. 'Embarrassment' suggests a minor irritant, which this is not. 'Mortification' is more like it, especially if we feel the word's allusion to death.

Every emotional episode is a particular event, with its own features. Our standard labels often have to be applied on a best fit basis. But there are ingredients that fall into standard patterns, as I have been indicating. Besides emotions that fall between the patterns for which we have standard labels, there are states that combine two or more emotions. One can feel regret that one did not feel shame, or shame that one is so easily embarrassed, and so on. There are so many possibilities.

Gaps in the pattern: shame versus guilt

We can feel guilt, too, as well as remorse and shame. All three are different. Guilt is in some ways between remorse and shame but has its own characteristics. It is like shame in that one takes oneself to be the object of an external critically judging point of view. And it is like remorse in that the judgement is of a specific act. You can feel vague shame for the general tone of your conduct, but not guilt. You can feel shame for having tried to do something wrong, and failed. (You might feel shame for the failure as well as for the intention if you are a particularly shame-prone person: silly fool couldn't even pull off a good fraud.) But guilt has to be for a wrong that actually occurred. Yet it is unlike remorse in that the criticism need not focus on the harm to individuals. We can feel guilty for harmless lies and betrayals of principles. There is a bias towards violations of rules where guilt is concerned, rather than betrayals of values or harm to persons. Suppose, for example, that on impulse you break into a friend's apartment when they are on holiday. You hope to find evidence showing that they are not the one who has been sending you nasty anonymized emails. You find evidence, leave everything unchanged, and depart. Later you feel guilty. Not for any harm, not for distrusting your friend (though you may also feel shame for that), but just for having done something one should not do, having broken the rule 'leave people's space alone'.

Two more complications. One is that we can feel guilt for very small transgressions. (In everyday interaction some people are good at making us feel guilty for these.) But we associate the word 'remorse' with serious harms to others. As a result, when the crime and the feeling are small, we prefer to describe the feeling as 'guilt' rather than 'remorse', even when it has the general pattern of remorse, because otherwise we seem to be over-stating it. The other is that guilt has an element of apprehension about it: waiting to be caught or accused. So we can contrast the present point of view in paradigm scenarios of shame – someone sees you sinning – and the past point of view in paradigm scenarios of remorse – you have hurt someone – with the future point of view in paradigm scenarios of guilt – a judgement on your crime will be pointed at you before long.

The pattern of guilt, as a moral emotion, is this. The person has an attitude of fear and respect towards a point of view, sometimes a future point of view, from which the person's specific breach of a rule on a particular occasion is noticed. As a result, actions that make amends to the real or imagined occupant of the point of view are salient. The distinguishing themes are thus that there is an element of fear in the attitude to the point of view, that a rule has been broken with a particular act, and that the point of view may be taken to be in the future.

These themes are independent of one another. As a result, when we contrast guilt with shame or remorse, we may be focusing on several aspects. And we may be at a loss for words when considering emotions which illustrate some but not all of the themes. To sum up the possible lines of contrast, here is a table, using labels that maximize the differences between the attitudes.

	target	attitude to point of view	attitude from point of view	temporal relation
shame	betrayal of value	admiration	contempt	to present
remorse	harm to person	empathy	appeal	to past
guilt	breach of rule	fear	anger	to future

But the particular emotion a person has on a particular occasion may not fit neatly along any one row. Some examples. Consider an emotion that is like guilt in that a rule has been broken, but like remorse in that there is an unanswerable appeal from a past point of view. You reveal someone's confidential admission at their funeral, and later feel them as pleading with you to respect your promise of silence. We might call this rule-directed remorse (or just ru(l)efulness). Or consider an emotion that is like guilt in that a rule has been broken, but like shame in that the attitude from the imagined point of view is contempt or ridicule rather than anger or condemnation. You imagine your Kantian mentor learning that you told a lie in order to mislead someone stalking your sister, and dismissing you as someone incapable of finding the options that would have made this unnecessary. Or consider an emotion that is like remorse in that someone has been hurt, and occupies the victim's point of view, but is like guilt or shame in that the attitude from that point of view is not appeal but condemnation or contempt. A legal analogue might be contempt of court: you tell a joke at the judge's expense. For a moral case, suppose you tell a story in public that deeply offends your parents, and then your emotion focuses not on their complaint but on their conclusion that you are a child who will bring such pain on its elders. We might call this empathetic guilt.

Continuing, consider an emotion that is like remorse in that the attribution of someone's pain to you resonates with you, but is so slight that remorse seems the wrong word for it. You step on someone's toe in the elevator, and an hour later find yourself wincing, 'Ooh, that must have hurt!' We might call this trivial remorse, or victim-directed guilt. Or consider an emotion that is like remorse in that a victim appeals to you in imagination, but is like guilt in that the point of view is from the future. The obvious examples are pathological but not impossible: you are planning a mugging and are haunted by the anticipated distress of your victim. We might call this anticipatory remorse. There can be cases where decent people feel something similar. You are a lawyer administering an estate and in order to get the rightful benefits to the inheritors you have to arrange for the eviction of squatters from a house, including a mother and infant who will have nowhere else to live. While you are signing the papers, the imagined eyes of this family stare at you. This might be anticipatory remorse, but given its similarity to the regret of agents in Williamsian moral dilemmas, we might also call it forward-looking regret.

Two kinds of pride

Pride has two contrasting opposites. On the one hand pride can be contrasted with humility: arrogant, vain, hubristic versus unassuming, moderate, reserved. On the other hand pride can be contrasted with shame: satisfied or self-respecting versus abashed or humiliated. In fact, there are two emotions here, which we run together under the same name. We might call them self-regard (or self-esteem) and self-respect. We can see this by asking whether pride is a virtue or a vice. It is a virtue in that we want people to have a good opinion of themselves, especially when it is deserved. It is a vice in that we do not want people to lord it over others or think they have greater rights than others. The conflict or confusion is illustrated by our attempts to translate Aristotle's account of 'pride'. There is a quality, he says in the *Nichomachean Ethics*, that grand and successful people have which on the one hand is a mean between undue humility and empty vanity, and on the other hand entails being an admirable person. Call it 'pride' for a moment. In this sense, though you can have more or less pride than you deserve, you cannot have too much deserved pride, and the truly admirable man is extremely proud. If we take this as our concept of pride, we think of Aristotle as admiring an overbearing, arrogant, display-orientated ideal person whom we would find unbearable. A better response is to see that 'pride' is a misleading translation, though Aristotle's concept is a variant on ours. His concept is much like our concept of self-respect, the opposite of shame, taken with a belief that self-respect requires impressive and demonstrative display from which we are now culturally distanced, in part by the influence of Christianity.

I shall try to explain the two concepts in ways that keep them distinct. First, self-regard. The simplest form is just admiration of oneself, as if from an external point of view. A slightly more complicated version is favourable comparison of oneself with others, admiring oneself more than others, as if comparing two other people. Then there is imagining an admired or revered point of view from which one is admired, congratulated, recommended, or whatever. The point of view is a human social one, usually within the norms of one's own society, and the attitude to it is one that you would have to a real person or group. This is different in that the point of view is itself the bearer of a particular imagined emotion. These emotions usually focus on some particular topic: someone is proud of their good looks, intelligence, or accomplishment. There can be some emotional cheating, when the significance of this topic is exaggerated or the comparison with others is unfair, and then self-regard fades into smugness. So I shall take the central case of self-regard to be where one imagines one's own society praising one for some particular act or quality.

(Then there is Hume's tricky problem of pride in something that is not oneself, for example at a grandchild's achievements. This seems common for self-regard and less so for self-respect. On my approach this amounts to imagining a point of view from which an approving gaze is directed at once at one oneself and at the thing one is proud of. One's identification with the other amounts to taking some imagined attitudes to it to be automatically directed at oneself as well. It is as if the targets were aligned, so that approval of the ultimate object had to pass through approval of oneself. So although it would be insane, there is no reason why someone might not feel a glow of pride when Mars is brighter in the sky than Venus, taking Mars to be his planet and imagining an authoritative observer to approve of his planet being the brighter one. I will say no more about this.)

Pride as self-respect is different. Someone hints that you have had very little passion in your life and you say, 'Nothing to be ashamed of there: no divorces, no breakdowns, no heartbreaks. In fact I'm proud of how little anguish I have been party to.' Your attitude need have no element of display about it, and no sense of comparison with others. You are postulating a point of view from which your life is acceptable and even to be preferred to a more adventurous one, but it may be an unconventional or hypothetical point of view.

Self-respect is an opposite of shame-guilt-remorse. I think that to make self-respect contrast most with self-regard we oppose it to guilt or remorse. Then one is imagining a fairly abstract point of view from which an attitude, for example love or acceptance, is directed at the person's life as a whole, extended through time. This can go with thinking, 'No one gets it completely right, we all make big mistakes, but this is good enough,' leaving it open which topics others handle better or how one stands in some overall ranking. It is even possible, I think, to reconcile self-respect with a low overall ranking of oneself, as long as there is some particular feature for which one would be approved of, perhaps loved.

Self-respect contrasts less sharply with self-regard if we take the alternative to be shame. Then the imagined point of view is a contemporary social attitude to something particular about one. This makes it crucial whether the attitude is represented as being that of actual other people, placing one in the social ranking of one's actual society, or a potential, abstract, or timeless one. If the former, we are in the territory of self-esteem or self-regard again, for then pride is a protection against social humiliation. This is an important point, because the need to protect against humiliation is associated with a tendency to violent behaviour. If you think that your status is very important and vulnerable, you are likely to react fiercely to threats to it. Julien Deonna and co-authors call this 'shame-proneness'. This kind of shame and this kind of pride are clearly parallel emotions.

Shame is the pivot that links these two different emotions. Shame as unlinked from the attitudes of actual people can be reversed as self-respect, as can the other members of the regret family. Shame as tied to actual attitudes is the reverse of self-esteem, and has a symbiotic relationship with it, so that fear of shame makes a need for pride-acknowledging signs of respect.

It is interesting that we have a less rich vocabulary for talking about positive attitudes to oneself than for talking about negative ones. I have separated self-respect and self-esteem, going somewhat beyond what is explicit in the language, and we could make more distinctions here, tracing out a more varied set of labels. But this would be going against a general tendency we have, of making more distinctions between kinds of disapproval than of approval. We have the emotions of distaste, disdain, critical feeling, disagreement, anger, dislike, hatred, contempt, condemnation, dismay, disgust, abhorrence, revulsion, and horror, and then on the other side we have the much shorter list of permissive, encouraging, pleased, and enthusiastic emotions. No doubt both lists can be extended, but the first will remain longer. One reason is that we have a conception of normal required behaviour and we assume that most people most of the time follow it. So we don't remark on it in others or congratulate ourselves on exhibiting it. But deviations from it, fallings short, are remarked on, and people have the unpleasantness of shame or remorse to goad them into compliance. This background conception may be a myth: ordinary cooperation and concern varies between people and in any person from occasion to occasion, so there may be more use for an emotion reflecting on even an ordinary good deed than folk wisdom allows.

The smug family

There's Grandma Smug, who sits on the porch in her underwear plus Sunday hat and cackles at the poor dress of everyone who goes by. There's Grandpa Smug, who walks around the garden looking at the neighbours' houses with binoculars to find cracks in their foundations. Mummy Smug holds her babies lovingly to her breast to protect them from the ugly people outside, and Daddy Smug lays traps for intruders, salespeople, and deliverers, because some of these folk are dangerous. Meanwhile Junior Smug goes on line and basks in the approval of his buddies, while holding his family in contempt, for they are filled with hate.

We don't make fine distinctions with words that we just throw out for their impact. But there are many kinds of smugness. There is the well-earned moral self-respect of someone who has avoided temptations and pitfalls to which others have succumbed. There is the self-deceived hypocritical smugness of someone who bolsters his vulnerable pride with asymmetrical comparisons with others. There is the tidy smugness of someone who seizes on one virtue among thousands and wraps herself in it against all criticism. There are many others. In this section I explore similarities between this family and that of regret, remorse, shame, and their cousins. The comparison ignores a lot, but it does bring out some connections between valuable capacities to have memotions such as remorse and disapproval and less wonderful memotions such as those of smugness and priggery.

There is an important distinction to make first. The other side of the smugness label is self-respect. People need to be able to describe to themselves the ways in which they ought to be valued and give themselves credit for doing well where others have failed. Smugness from the outside, deserved self-respect from the inside. So it matters what kind of smugness we are talking of when we discuss soiled memotions, for some people have earned some kinds while others are faults.

Contrast four lines for securing one's self-respect:

(a) *I'm decent because the ones I respect approve of me. (My acts on this occasion were acceptable because these authorities do not disapprove.)* The parallel with shame is obvious. Self-respect is gained through a respected point of view. A bad attitude from that point of view would be shaming for the person. This smugness is a kind of moral snobbery.

(b) *I'm decent because I have broken no rule.* The parallel is with guilt: no condemnation comes from some point of view eligible to judge the person. If we need a name for this, let us call this the smug protestation of innocence.

(c) *I'm decent because I have caused no culpable harm.*
The parallel is with remorse. No victim condemns
the person; no respected point of view keeps bringing the injury to one's attention. Someone may be
hurt, and it may be regrettable, but it is not one's
fault. Let us call this teflon smugness.

(d) *I'm decent because there is nothing I need to reconsider.* The parallel is with regret. The person is not
haunted by their acts and attitudes, in the way that
they would be with guilt, shame, and remorse. This
smugness is often best called complacency.

Let me say more about the last of these. There is
always something one could well be rethinking, from
the balance between honesty and kindness to the question of what this morality business is all about. So
everyone who is not in a constant agony of critical self-
examination is vulnerable to the charge of not rethinking
enough. It's like an existentialist charge of inauthentic-
ity: you can't escape it. It is particularly inescapable
because you can examine your thinking and motives on
the wrong topics, as well in the wrong amounts. You
can be constantly worrying about whether your attitude
to gender issues is correct, but be told you are too blithe
about global injustice. And you can fake rethinking
without knowing it, so it's hard to be sure that you
are doing real fundamental rethinking on the areas
that really matter. But when the topic is a particular
event, when the concern is more with a specific emotion
than a general mood, things can be more definite. You
can be smugly blind to the flaws in your behaviour to
colleagues, as you hear the sobs emanating from the
washroom, while not being smug about your treatment

of important mentors, which you are constantly revisiting and never satisfied with.

The inescapability is the most interesting thing here. Everyone needs self-respect, and yet attempts to preserve or defend it can be charged with smugness, sometimes fairly. One reason is an easy slide in little increments: from self-respect to lack of shame to self-regard to smugness. If you have done nothing wrong, you have done nothing wrong: your smug protest of innocence is justified. But your teflon assurance that you have harmed nobody may be more fragile: it is easy to hurt while breaking no moral rule. Moral snobbery carries the least weight. That is, if one's claim to be a better person than those around one is based *just* on the opinions of one's favoured judges, then there is force to the charge of smugness. But it is also worrying if someone's self-respect is based entirely on her own assessment of her conduct, in opposition to the opinion of others: a moral individualist whose confidence that she has broken no rules and needs rethink nothing is based on her own thoughts and emotions alone. The most worrying aspect would be the refusal to think that in the face of the opinion of respected authorities she doesn't have a reason to reconsider her own judgement. This is a different kind of smugness: indifferent to shame and self-armoured against remorse.

Because real memotions are important, we have to defend ourselves against the fake ones. We have to identify the particular attitudes that we think of as smug, and react to with criticism or derision (or, very often, with teasing, which the truly smug do not even notice). It is not easy, there are no simple formulas. Thus we have to nudge one another and fine-tune our emotions and thinking, so that we react in suitable ways to suitable versions of smugness. But that challenges other people's self-respect: to secure it they must have some manner of satisfaction that in general and on particular topics what they do is worthy of approval. A little mild moral snobbery does no harm, but too much and too easy blocks our questioning of one another. Protestations of innocence are fine for the innocent, but we can protest too much. Teflon is useful, but doesn't earn trust. Some complacency is inevitable, but we have to press one another to revisit issues that we would like to think settled. Can better labels and a bit of geography make it easier to feel our way through this maze?

Dark humour, radical possibilities

You are about to be murdered by a gang of drugged-up teenagers. You expect it will be slow and horrible. Of course, you think they shouldn't do it; that's an understatement. You think that any reasonable person would react with horror. But you find a remarkable absence of anger at them. This is what is going to happen, and you wish it were not, and it will be their fault. But it is more like falling into the way of a pack of wolves than like being betrayed by someone you trusted. And it is an awful fact about your society that it turns children into wolves. You take it as a deep and hard-to-change fact about human nature that this can happen. Looking at the alert, somehow innocent, but not-quite-there faces of the teenagers, you are reminded of the dogs behind your neighbour's fence, bored and aggressive, watching dogs, cats, and rabbits in the park across the road. You can imagine the steady tail wag that fierce dogs sometimes have. You hear a laugh within yourself, though no sound comes out of your mouth. You had thought there was some difference between you and a rabbit.

Sometimes one can see the dark humour in one's situation, and in human life generally, and much of the time one cannot. You, in the example, will be in a position to have a disapproval-type attitude to the horrors that are about to occur. But you can see them in two unusual ways. First as ridiculous, as people acting as people always have, in contradiction to their own long-term interests, for reasons they do not understand, undermining the pretensions of the whole species to be capable of organized life. One of the elements of this attitude is the conflict between two juxtaposed points of view: one seeing the acts as diverting and even exciting, and the other seeing them as a dreary routine in miserable lives. So the acts are shameful, but in the way of being ridiculous, in a way comic. In fact, they don't have to seem comic in a direct way for the emotion to apply. If one can just see how this point of view is possible, one is appreciating the awful sad comic possibilities. One would also feel horror, fear, and disgust. These might be the basis of another attitude of condemnation. Or they might not: one could take the absurdity-based attitude as the one that an objective point of view would fasten on. All in the five minutes left.

The other attitude you may have is despair at the chances of making fine furniture from this warped wood, to paraphrase Kant. Despair at these children and the whole atrocious species. Despair is the emotion that recognizes the futility of hope. Framing the situation this way can provide the base for another evaluative attitude. Criticism goads us into better behaviour, and is based on the hope that a regular pattern of behaviour is possible. Criticism is also expressive, releasing and sublimating the annoyance or anger that bad behaviour provokes. But in awful situations the amount of anger that would be proportional to what we feel in merely bad situations is more than we can feel. It would burn up the world. So the usual bases of criticism are pointless. Instead we can incorporate despair into our criticism, since disapproval is a moral attitude with a lot of freedom about what emotion goes into its 'from' slot. The attitude then is that from a point of view one aspires to, the act in question evokes despair, the failures of this individual showing the hopelessness of the species.

How widely could we have this attitude? We do have mild versions of it every day. If your dog is ruining his digestion by an addiction to horse poop, which he rushes to find whenever he is off the leash, you disapprove and tell him off. But in your heart you know he is incurable, so it is a disapproval of sadness rather than of anger. If your five-year-old child is always singing when she should be getting dressed, you sigh and chide. But your annoyance is tinged with resignation. We know that many things resist change, and that expressing specifically moral disapproval is often counterproductive. So when the stakes are very low our disapproval is often loaded with resignation rather than anger. Sometimes it makes sense that it should be when the stakes are very high, too.

The two attitudes, absurdity and despair, are cousins. Certainly one could load one's disapproval with either one and not the other. But they prepare the ground for each another. It is part of the absurdity of human life that with such high aspirations we fail so frequently, and for such trivial reasons. It is a reason for despair that there cannot be a noble story acted by clowns such as us. The two combine easily when we move from attitudes of disapproval to self-evaluative attitudes. There is a kind of existential pride in maintaining one's comparisons while accepting the lack of an ultimate standard of evaluation. (Accepting that some things are much more important than others, from the perspective that we use most of the time, and that there is a perspective from which all our plans and accomplishments are uniformly absurd.) There is a kind of remorse that consists in attention to the point of view from which all your best attempts are seen as ridiculous in the typical human way. (Like remorse, because the incurability of the species is like the unchangeability of the past.) It is a remorse that is tied to despair, but it is not real unless it can also lead to a wry chuckle.

There is a thread of literature that resonates to this, always a minority and offensive to some, telling us that some things are too awful to be taken seriously. From a generation ago there is the Peter de Vries novel *The Blood of the Lamb*, and a few years ago there is the Roberto Benigni film *Life is Beautiful*. There have been other more recent light treatments of Holocaust and terrorism themes; it would be a misunderstanding to think that they are condoning what they have fun with. And most of Samuel Beckett can be seen as an attempt to combine the comic and the despairing, working for a kind of sombre guffaw that comes into its own when the themes are life, death, and sanity.

Shaping our emotions

You can't just decide to be happy, or to have some chosen belief. And if you are experiencing self-punishing remorse when regret would make more sense, it is not enough simply to tell yourself so. This is true on a collective level, too. Suppose your whole society is prone to violent condemnation of some acts when it would be better if instead you could all be sad or amused or just shrug your shoulders. Then your solitary voice saying this may not have any effect, not even on your own attitudes.

But we should not conclude that we have no power over what we can feel. Compare physical movements. You can move a finger by deciding to. You can also move your whole body to Paris. But just gritting your teeth and saying with determination 'Paris, Paris, Paris' won't do it. You have to buy a plane ticket, get yourself to the airport, and so on. Most things that we can do are of this second kind: we have to do other things in order to do them. That includes changing our states of mind. We can make ourselves believe things, by attending selectively to evidence and choosing whom we associate with, though it can be very difficult if the belief is absurd, and sometimes defeats the point of believing. We can make ourselves want things, though making yourself want vomit-flavoured ice-cream would be very difficult, besides being a stupid thing to do. And we can make ourselves experience emotions, though sometimes it is difficult and sometimes it would not be a sensible thing to do. The difficulty can approach practical impossibility, but we often simply do not know whether an emotion would be easy or difficult to acquire.

I will give three reasons why having the concept of a particular moral emotion – having it in a full way by having a word for it, being able to describe cases where people experience it, and being able to imagine having it – makes it easier to enter into the emotion.

The first reason applies to other emotions, too. It is just attention. If we have a name for a pattern of behaviour, then we are more likely to notice it when it occurs, and having noticed it, we are in a better position to imagine being in a state that would lead to it, and being able to imagine it, we are nearer to being able to enter into it. As argued in part I, emotions have characteristic pressures, and to imagine the pressure is to be in a state similar to the emotion. This is one way that unconscious emotions become conscious, simply by having their consequences gathered into one frame. The same process can assist a transition from latent possibility to imaginability to experience.

An example – based on an overheard philosophico-literary conversation of Peter Goldie's – is retrospective jealousy. Someone has no idea that one might be jealous of people one's partner was involved with before knowing one. Then she reads a work of fiction in which someone experiences the emotion (such as Julian Barnes' *Before She Knew Me* or, from another age, Edith Wharton's *The Reef*). At first she is puzzled, but struggles to make sense of the characters' attitudes. As she succeeds, she notices in her own case the opportunities for the emotion and the ways it would lead her to act. Then to her surprise she begins to identify it in herself, as a characteristic feeling, set of concerns, and tendencies to action. She says that the glimmerings of the emotion were always there, but that now it has become a disturbing factor in her life.

The second reason is specific to moral emotions. It is the availability of the components of the emotions. If you understand anger and respect, then you can understand disapproval, taking it as respect for a point of view from which anger is directed at something. You can do this *if* you understand what it is to imagine a point of view to which and from which an emotion is directed, something I take to be a basic human capacity, though more developed in some than in others. So with moral emotions we have a fixed frame of points of view, which needs just to have different basic emotions attached to it. Some points of view are themselves easy to grasp (particular or imaginary people), and others require some help from one's culture (the ancestors, God, ideal impartial observers). But what difficulties there are here lie in acquiring the concepts rather than finding one's way into the emotions.

The third reason is the vividness and emotional resonance of our imagination of people. An angry parental figure, a cool dispassionate impartial judge: these are images that are easy to summon, and make it easy to feel oneself as objects of their interest, concern, approval, or disgust. The concept of the memotion tells one what personalities to imagine, in which roles in the perspective structure of the emotion. When the points of view are more abstract or far-removed, or more subtle (such as that of the sad and ironical kind-yet-humorous contrarian that could be summoned in seeing the absurdity of life), the images are less vivid, and imagining them may have less emotional force. One response is to fictionalize personalities onto them, perhaps with theological or historical trimmings. The formula is simple: we want the description to produce an emotion, as vivid as we can, rather than some pale intellectual substitute, and so we supply a real graspable personality to occupy the point of view. Then reactions to the personality can give colour to the emotions. (Note, going back to part II, that in imagining the personality, what we have to do is imagine not so much a way a real person could be, but rather a combination of features that fit easily into our person-imagining capacities, as fictional characters do.)

I am describing a way of making moral emotions available, by giving them attention, grasping their perspective structure, and imagining occupants of their points of view. I think that this is a route that we often take, both in little individual shifts of emotional repertoire and in larger cultural changes. I will illustrate it with an example. The example concerns the familiar contrast between unhelpful guilt and necessary regret. I should start with a disclaimer: this is meant not as advice on how to make emotional transitions, or a recipe for therapy, but as an analysis of what is happening when an emotion becomes available, and an explanation of how this is possible.

The example is a case of survivor guilt. Suppose that a person is the only survivor of a shooting in which a sniper picks off all of her companions, one by one, in front of her eyes. She only survives by chance: the sniper's gun jammed and while he was reloading he noticed a wounded person move. He shot that person and then was killed by a police marksman. Our person, like many in these circumstances, feels as if her survival is bought at the expense of her companions' deaths, so that she is to blame for surviving. She may not believe the irrational thoughts that go with this emotion; she knows that they are false, but she can feel the pressure towards them. It is an emotion that is sure to cause the person unnecessary damage and distress. It is unnecessary in that there are less harmful things to feel, which do equal justice to the tragedy.

It makes a difference what the guilty emotion is, in more detail, from what perspective what attitude is directed. I will discuss only guilt that centres on the thought 'It isn't fair that I survived; it's at the cost of the deaths of my companions.' One possibility is that the person imagines her dead companions wanting life, and resenting her for having the life they crave. (Similarly, people with fatal diseases can resent others who will survive them.) So she feels their anger directed at her, as if they want something she has, life. A second possibility is that she imagines a love for each of the victims, as if from a god-like or mothering figure who wants to give life to them but cannot because it has been taken by her. The thought here is of an arbitrary and unfair distribution of fates, in which she has somehow cheated and come out ahead. A third possibility, perhaps the simplest, imagines the point of view of a judge of her worth, who asks whether she has a greater claim to survive than the others and concludes that she does not. If she survived with no greater claim, then she must have illegitimately pushed herself ahead of the others.

These are different, and they are not the only possibilities. Simply saying 'guilt for being the survivor' misses the important details. The imagined points of view are different, as are the attitudes directed at the person from them. These differences are linked to different forms of regret which could take their places. In each case begin by shifting the way the occupant of the point of view is imagined. In the first case – anger from the victims – the natural shift to make is from thinking of them solely in terms of life or death. What else did they want, what else can we imagine them wanting if they could know what had happened? They will have cared for particular causes and for particular people, so their unfocused lust for survival can be compared to the unfulfilled, but not unfulfillable, desire that these causes be furthered and these people helped. Anger becomes sadness. My strong intuition is that this shift would be easier given a vivid focus on the actual personalities of particular victims, rather than seeing them as, say, 'the fifty who died when I did not', asking the real question of what *they* would be asking for.

The second case – resentment from a loving attitude to the victims – is likely to involve thoughts both from an impersonal point of view and from a more individual human one. We could imagine a god who loved the victims, whose deaths were against Her will. The shift then would be to the god's love for the survivor, too, and ways that that love could be vindicated. The survivor can make herself be loved for a purpose, to accomplish some end. Resentment becomes hope, perhaps a desperate hope against the odds, but also one that motivates a push to make something of one's life. Or we could imagine the actual people who loved the victims and are confused by the fact that someone they were not close to is the survivor. But the more we take them as real people, the more we see them as in need of comfort, and their attitude as dismay and confusion rather than anger. The regretful feeling of sharing their mourning is very different from imagining resentment.

In the third case – contempt from a judge watching over human fate – a rather different transformation is possible. The judge's attention is on the unworthiness of the survivor. This is hard to deflect, as the more anyone reflects, the more of their own failings they see. So instead of turning away from it, we can turn towards it, and think of all the ways in which the survivor has not lived up to hopes. But then everyone else has failed and disappointed, too – at least they would have from the perspective of such an impersonal judge. So the movement is in the direction of universal despair rather than individual contempt. What form this can take – dark irony about the pretensions of humanity, resolve to rescue something of value from the wreckage, a commitment to managing the awful in human life – depends on the ways in which the imagined judge can be made vivid to the survivor, and then transformed. But in any case guilt has now turned into a profound regret. Not anything like a superficial wish that the tragedy had not occurred, but a despairing recognition of its enormity and a project of rehearsing events to see how else they might have unfolded. This might eventually transform itself into an interest in gun control, in the identification of dangerous people, and in research into the histories that lead to such dangerousness.

End: a virtue of imagination

It is often hard to grasp the attitudes of well-meaning reasonable people. One reason is the enormous range of emotions people can have when they imagine points of view and frame more basic emotions on them. So there is an imaginative skill, of imagining not just how things seem from others' points of view, but what points of view others are imagining and structuring their emotions around. Imagining others' emotional use of their imagination. It is an important virtue. Explaining why, in this final section, will bring together several themes that have threaded through the book: imagination, emotion, points of view, the variety of moral emotions, the closeness of admirable and disreputable moral emotions.

The idea is positive: there is a virtue we should cultivate. It complements two rather radical negative ideas that have emerged. The first is that there are no *emotions* of moral approval and disapproval, shorn of their components of anger, disgust, encouragement, admiration, and so on, shaped over the frame of imagined points of view.

End: a virtue of imagination

In arguing for this earlier – towards the end of the section 'Emotional learning' in part III – I focused on cases where you experience emotions that undermine your earlier disapproval, so that you no longer had respect or affection for its point of view. I argued that the disapproval would dissolve. But it would not dissolve if it had really been a simple unstructured emotion. The other is that less desirable moral emotions, notably those in the smug family, are inevitable consequences of the same processes that give us the memotions that make human social life possible. They are made of the same materials – arrogance and self-respect have similar blueprints – so that the question of which emotions we should encourage in one another can take some pretty subtle turns.

A person acts, moved by shame, approval, condemnation, or some other moral emotion. Another person tries to understand, and perhaps to anticipate the next action. But she knows that if *she* were acting from shame, approval, or condemnation, she would do something very different. Perhaps what he calls shame is leading him to public confession rather than wanting to hide; perhaps what he calls condemnation is leading him to teasing rather than attack. One possibility the second person must face is that his shame, or his condemnation, are not hers. Perhaps they are different emotions with some family resemblance. Part of the evidence that a similar but different emotion was at work could be that the second person managed to imagine such an emotion and it fitted. But to get this evidence, she would have to be able to do the imagining.

Imagining the other person's emotion here means imagining their imagination, and it is no different from other cases we have seen. The point now is that it is an important and sophisticated virtue, something we can gain from learning and encouraging. Call it the virtue of imaginative rebundling, because it requires us to take the pieces from which our own moral emotions are constructed and rebundle them as an approximation to someone else's. It is different from the virtue of being able to see things from another person's point of view. It has an extra twist: it is being able to see things from a point of view that the other imagines, and then to follow through with a grasp of how this influences the other person's emotions. It is also different from the virtue of tolerating other people's differing moral opinions. Simple tolerance means taking what people approve, disapprove, admire, or condemn at face value, and living with the fact that these are not exactly your attitudes to the same things. Rebundling means something more subtle, since you have to get your head around how others have different attitudes, which could be mistaken for yours, to the same and to different objects.

This can happen with moral approval and disapproval, where, for example, one person's attitude to someone eating meat imagines sadness from the perspective of nature, another's imagines fury from the perspective of a giver of rules for human conduct, and a third's imagines indifference also from the perspective of a law-giver for humanity. It seems as if the first and second agree – they both disapprove – and both disagree with the third. But the second and the third may have more in common, both coming from a law-giver's perspective, even though differing in what is seen from that point of view. Or for a rather different example consider the gulf between two people when one builds his self-respect on the imagined encouragement of powerful authority figures and the other on imagined appreciation by the benevolent but pessimistic point of view of posterity. (From the first perspective the slogan is 'Be grand; never seem inferior', and from the second it is 'Don't fake it; never seem pretentious'. But for both it is a matter of integrity.) So 'arrogant bully' meets 'ridiculous softie'. They will take completely different funerals as honouring a deceased. Each may be puzzled: 'Why do they need *that* for self-respect?' But emotional unbundling would show them that they have different respects for different selves.

It's an anti-smug virtue. At any rate it tends against one kind of smugness, one that particularly preys on people – like me! – who suspect that other people's views about right and wrong are primitive and confused. We think, 'Yes, she is of the sincere opinion that that was a terrible thing to do, but her feeling of disapproval, well, it's just a mixture of the hostilities she thinks her mother would have and the disappointment she imagines that God would have, so there's no attempt to sense what an impartial reflective view of the situation would be.' Perhaps there is no such attempt, and perhaps it would be better if our moral emotions did show such attempts; but that does not prevent the disapproval being a properly moral emotion, seeing a situation from a per-spective of authority which might coordinate the actions of different people. Not to unbundle emotionally is not to see this, and is a smugness that people like the author of this book are particularly prone to. It is to confuse the question 'Is this a moral emotion?' with the question 'Is it desirable that this emotion be widespread?' Though imagination shapes emotion, it cannot tell us which emotions we would benefit from having.

Notes

Part I

Refined emotions   Continuities – 'homology' – between simple biologically based and socially shaped emotions are discussed in Clark (2010). Holodynski and Friedlmeier (2006) describes ways in which the individual's coping with social demands can lead to these continuities. Chapter 11 of Fox (2008) warns against taking emotions as determined by fixed biological factors. I worry about brain imaging in the study of emotion that our present technology has only crude temporal resolution, so it can miss rapidly changing activations of several areas, as most likely with the emotions I am most interested in.

Imagining in emotion   For standard and influential accounts of imagination see Gendler (2011), Kind (2001). See chapter 1 of McGinn (2004) and chapter 1 of Currie and Ravenscroft (2002) for the differences between imagination and belief. Currie and Ravenscroft make a useful distinction between the creative imagination, the capacity for novel and even impossible mental creations, and the recreative imagination, which represents mentally things that in fact exist. And it is important that for them imagined emotions are emotions. See Harris (2000) on imagination in children and human life generally. Gibert (2012) discusses the role of the imagination in moral life. For similarities between humans and other mammals in the structures underlying emotion see chapter 1 of Fox (2008). For more on emotions of non-human animals see Tappolet (2010). Motor images are discussed in Jeannerod (1995). Aglioti and others (1995) make it clear that motor images are different from perceptual images. An early observation that emotions filter information and options by making some more salient than others is in de Sousa (1987). Chapters 5 and 6 of Williamson (2007) defend the idea that imagination can be a reliable source of knowledge under certain conditions.

Emotions and thinking   The central reading has to be Damasio (2004). See also Stocker (2004), Schmitt and Lahroodi (2008), and Morton (2010a). Brady (2011) argues that there is an epistemic dimension to most emotion, in that emotions pressure one to find out if they are well founded.

Keeping mood and emotion distinct   Ratcliffe (2008) is very explicit about the distinction between mood and emotion. See also Tappolet (2010). The essential reading on emotion in music is Kivy (1989); also Robinson (2010). See Deonna and Teroni (2012) for a novel take on the differences between emotions, moods, and temperaments.

Pressure Accounts of emotion which link emotions more closely to belief are found in Soloman (1993) and Nussbaum (2001). The difficulties these have with irrational emotions are discussed in Greenspan (1988). Greenspan describes emotions as exerting pressures on other states, which she takes usually to be accompanied by conscious and sometimes unpleasant sensations. The related idea of scenarios or scripts for emotions is discussed in de Sousa (1987) and Goldie (2000). Kaster (2005) uses the script idea to discuss an alien set of emotions, those of ancient Rome. Chapter 6 of Fox (2008) reports studies of the effects of emotion on perception.

Categories of emotion Rorty (1982) is a classic attempt to unravel passions, emotions, and sentiments in the history of European thought. Schmitter (2013) is a more recent view of part of the same territory. Stoic views are discussed in Nussbaum (2001), Braund and Gilbert (2003), and Braund and Gill (2007). In Kaster (2005) Roman emotions are largely identified by corresponding virtues. Morton (2002a) discusses the relation between emotions and virtues. The relation between emotions, moods, and traits of character is discussed in Goldie (2004).

Part II

Imagining what we shouldn't feel The issues here are related to questions of 'imaginative resistance', questions of why it is hard to imagine something wrong being right. These are discussed in section 5 of Gendler (2011), and in Walton (2006). The issues in part II connect with questions of the motives for evil actions, on which there is a large literature, to which my contribution is Morton (2004).

Imagining minds: emotions and perspectives Issues about our knowledge of other people's minds have been in philosophy for ages, and in the past decades many philosophers and psychologists have shared an interest in 'mindreading' or the use of a 'theory of mind'. Some of this work is summarized in Morton (2009a). To emphasize imagination rather than attribution in general inclines us towards 'simulation' accounts. See Davies and Stone (1995). The immediacy of others' emotions in our experience is a theme of the tradition that takes an emotion to be a perception of a value. See Tappolet (2000). The relation between a picture and whatever it depicts has received a lot of attention, some of which is summarized in Walton (1990).

Imagining a point of view See Goldie (2000) for perspective in imagination. For narrative structure in fiction and its connection with imaginative perspective see part II of Currie (1995). Reactions to fictions as if they were real are discussed in Walton (1990). Human acuteness at picking up the perspectives of others' attention is a theme of much work in developmental psychology. See Carpenter and others (1988). Brunyé and others (2009) has a fascinating account of the link between pronoun use and perspective, and how imagined situations affect it. For Gordon's work on simulating the situation of another see Gordon (1995); the other chapters in Davies and Stone (1995) are also relevant. See also Goldman (2008) here.

Notes

Misimagination   This section is essentially the same as Morton (2006), with an allusion to the issues in Morton (2002b). Zaki and others (2009) is on the same topic from an experimental point of view. The classic empirical work on mistaken self-attribution is summarized in Nisbett and Ross (1980). For applications of it to issues similar to those discussed here see Nichols and Stich (2003). See Doris (2002) and chapter 3 of Goldie (2004) for discussions of the fragility of attributions of personality that connect with issues about literature.

Imagining invented characters: fiction and philosophy   The essential reading here is from Gregory Currie. See Currie (1995) and Currie (2011). See also chapter 8 of Doris (2002). The discussion of 'free indirect style' in Wood (2009) is all about subtle expressions of a fictional person's point of view. I know of no discussions of what descriptions of emotions correspond to things people actually feel, and I commend the topic. The worries I raise for myself here are somewhat like those which experimental philosophers raise for epistemology and ethics. See Knobe and Nichols (2008).

Invisible everyday failures   This is partly based on Morton (2010b). The connection with Heal (1995) was inspired by a remark by Madeleine Ransom. The explanation of barriers to imagining evil motivation is partly based on Morton (2011). A contrasting picture is in Kekes (2005).

Imagining awful actions   Barriers against violent and other atrocious actions are discussed in Morton (2004). Again a different picture is defended in Kekes (2005).

Sympathy versus empathy   The absolutely essential reading here is from Coplan and Goldie (2011a). In connection with this section see particularly Coplan and Goldie's introduction (2011b) and the chapters by Battaly, Goldie, and Matravers (all 2011). Steuber (2006) links early sociological work to late twentieth-century psychology and philosophy of mind. Deonna (2007) discusses the function of empathy in moral life.

The tradeoff   For the Knobe effect see Knobe (2008).

Part III

The threat of irrelevance   Essential reading on the new sentimentalism are Haidt (2001), Nichols (2004), Prinz (2007), and Kelly (2011). Converging on some similar conclusions from a different starting point is Zagzebski (2003). Maibom (2009) contests Nichols' claims about empathy, partly on empirical grounds.

A number of writers have defended the broadly Nietzschean suggestion that we might be better off if people's acts were not shaped by their sentiments of moral approval and disapproval. There are non-mainstream writers such as Ian Hinkfuss (1987) and Hans-Georg Moeller (2009). And there are a number of places in the writings of Bernard Williams where he warns us against taking Morality as a unified all-important thing that is inevitably good for us (see, especially, the last chapter of Williams, 1985). Complementary to this there are studies by Erik Schwitzgebel and others – see Schwitzgebel (2009) and Schwitzgebel and Rust (2009) – suggesting that the study of moral philosophy is at most neutral with respect to one's being someone that others will choose to cooperate with, and quite likely of negative value. Some general techniques for studying the spread of ideas, moral and other, are in Sperber (1996).

Retracting emotions   For related, but not identical, views, see Morton (2002b) and chapter 4 of de Sousa (2011). An important topic related to that of emotional retraction is forgiveness. See Calhoun (1992), Griswold (2007). I don't know how exactly to think of forgiveness as retraction.

Emotions with multiple points of view   Here the ideas of Taylor (1985) are prominent, though she might not approve of my use of them. It is worth pointing out that one can imagine one's own point of view, for example in mutual imagination when each of two people imagines the other imagining them. (Sometimes a smile communicates that this is happening.)

The variety of moral emotions   The statues of Epicurus are discussed in Alfano (2013), as is the experiment with watching eyes. Zimmerman (1993) defends the idea that there is nothing wrong with having conflicting moral attitudes. Large-scale cases analogous to the bear and garbage case are discussed in Morton (1996), and Morton (2002c) discusses the idea that people naturally tend to cooperative outcomes. Conflicts such as those between keeping order and encouraging childish character are discussed in Morton (2009a). Violence-inhibiting mechanisms are described in Nichols (2004). Vorauer and Sasaki (2009) has evidence that empathy can lead to hostility to strangers. The Pomnyun Sunim quotation can be found in several places, including Sang-hun

(2012). For Kohlberg's stages of moral development see Kohlberg (1981). Almost nobody believes that these are universal or that they represent unambiguous moral progress.

Smugness   The topic of smugness is present behind the scenes in much of Bernard Williams' writings, though he rarely uses the word. Jeffries (2002) is in part an interview in which Williams mentions smugness. Examples like the one in this section in which someone is overconfident about her own attitudes are suggested by remarks by Bernard Williams, in various places. See, for example, chapter 4, including its long first endnote, in Williams (1993). Grounds for a link between smugness and evil-facilitation are suggested in Morton (2009b). Less than wonderful emotions in general are discussed in Tappolet (2011).

Part IV

Shame, regret, embarrassment, remorse and *Shame-like versus regret-like*   The C. S. Lewis quote is the first sentence of *A Grief Observed* (1961). The essential reading on retrospective emotions is Taylor (1985) and Williams (1973, 1981, 1993). See also Rorty (1980), Bittner (1992), Dilman (1999), Maibom (2010), Deonna and others (2011 – the quotation in the text is from p. 136). I picked up the contrast between hostile observers and the unchangeable past from a remark by Elliot Goodine.

Ghosts   Dilman (1999) focuses on related issues.

Looking backward and looking inward and *Gaps in the pattern: shame versus guilt* I know of no literature on emotions that we might but do not feel. There is a lot written about emotions in other cultures; summarized in chapter 1 of Fox (2008). See also Shaver and others (1992). But there is very little in the form of links with the kind of structuring of our culture's emotions that I am discussing. One exception is discussion of emotions in the ancient Greek and Roman worlds; see Williams (1993), Braund and Most (2003), Kaster (2005), Braund and Gill (2007).

Two kinds of pride See Aristotle *Nichomachean Ethics*, book II, section 14, and book IV section 3, Hume *A Treatise of Human Nature*, book II, part 1. Also chapter 2 of Taylor (1985), Dilman (1999). For the connection between violence and shame-proneness see chapter 2 of Deonna and others (2011).

Shaping our emotions Sherman (2011) discusses survivor guilt, and in more scholarly form in Sherman (2005). Some of the factors that might appear in a re-focusing of guilt in which the victims' real voices appear are mentioned in Card (2002), especially chapters 7 and 9.

References

Aglioti, Salvatore, Melvyn A. Goodale, and Joseph F. X. DeSouza (1995) 'Size contrast illusions deceive the eye but not the hand', *Current Biology* 5, 679–85

Alfano, Mark (2013) *Character as Moral Fiction*, Cambridge: Cambridge University Press

Battaly, Heather (2011) 'Is empathy a virtue?', in Amy Coplan and Peter Goldie, eds, *Empathy: Philosophical and Psychological Perspectives*, Oxford: Oxford University Press, 277–301

Bittner, Rüdiger (1992) 'Is it reasonable to regret things one did?', *Journal of Philosophy* 89(5), 262–73

Brady, Michael (2011) 'Emotions, perceptions, and reasons', in Carla Bagnoli, ed., *Morality and the Emotions*, Oxford: Oxford University Press, 135–49

Braund, Susanna and Giles Gilbert (2003) 'An ABC of epic *ira*', in Susanna Braund and Glenn Most, eds, *Ancient Anger*, Cambridge: Cambridge University Press, 250–85

Braund, Susanna and Christopher Gill, eds (2007)

References

The Passions in Roman Thought and Literature, Cambridge: Cambridge University Press

Braund, Susanna and Glenn Most, eds (2003) *Ancient Anger,* Cambridge: Cambridge University Press

Brunyé, Tad, Tali Ditman, Caroline R. Mahoney, Jason S. Augustyn, and Holly A. Taylor (2009) 'When you and I share perspectives: pronouns modulate perspective taking during narrative comprehension', *Psychological Science* 20(1), 27–32

Calhoun, Cheshire (1992) 'Changing one's heart', *Ethics* 103(1), 76–96

Card, Claudia (2002) *The Atrocity Paradigm,* Oxford: Oxford University Press

Carpenter, Malinda, Katherine Nagell, and Michael Tomasello (1988) *Social Cognition and Communicative Competence from 8 to 15 Months of Age,* Chicago: University of Chicago Press

Clark, Jason (2010) 'Relations of homology between higher cognitive emotions and basic emotions', *Biology and Philosophy* 25, 75–94

Coplan, Amy and Peter Goldie, eds (2011a) *Empathy: Philosophical and Psychological Perspectives,* Oxford: Oxford University Press

Coplan, Amy and Peter Goldie (2011b) 'Introduction', in Amy Coplan and Peter Goldie, eds, *Empathy: Philosophical and Psychological Perspectives,* Oxford: Oxford University Press, ix–xlvii

Copp, David (2007) *Morality in a Natural World: Selected Essays in Metaethics,* Cambridge: Cambridge University Press

Currie, Gregory (1995) *Image and Mind,* Cambridge: Cambridge University Press

References

Currie, Gregory (2011) 'Let's pretend', *Times Literary Supplement* 21 September, 14–15

Currie, Gregory and Ian Ravenscroft (2002) *Recreative Minds*, Oxford: Oxford University Press

Damasio, Antonio (2004) *Descartes' Error: Emotion, Reason, and the Human Brain*, New York: Putnam

Davies, Martin and Tony Stone, eds (1995) *Mental Simulation: Evaluations and Applications*, Oxford: Blackwell

Deonna, Julien (2007) 'The structure of empathy', *Journal of Moral Philosophy* 4(1), 99–116

Deonna, Julien and Fabrice Teroni (2012) *The Emotions: A Philosophical Introduction*, London: Routledge

Deonna, Julien, Raffaele Rodogno, and Fabrice Teroni (2011) *In Defense of Shame: The Faces of an Emotion*, Oxford: Oxford University Press

de Sousa, Ronald (1987) *The Rationality of the Emotions*, Cambridge, MA: MIT Press

de Sousa, Ronald (2011) *Emotional Truth*, Oxford: Oxford University Press

Dilman, Ilham (1999) 'Shame, guilt and remorse', *Philosophical Investigations* 22, 312–29

Doris, John (2002) *Lack of Character*, Cambridge: Cambridge University Press

Fox, Elaine (2008) *Emotion Science*, Basingstoke: Palgrave Macmillan

Gendler, Tamar (2011) 'Imagination', in Edward N. Zalta, ed., *The Stanford Encyclopedia of Philosophy* (Fall Edition), *http://plato.stanford.edu/archives/fall2011/entries/imagination/* (accessed 7 January 2013)

Gibert, Martin (2012) 'Imagination et perception morale', Ph.D. thesis, Université de Montréal

References

Goldie, Peter (2000) *The Emotions: A Philosophical Exploration*, Oxford: Oxford University Press

Goldie, Peter (2004) *On Personality*, London: Routledge

Goldie, Peter (2011) 'Anti-empathy', in Amy Coplan and Peter Goldie, eds, *Empathy: Philosophical and Psychological Perspectives*, Oxford: Oxford University Press, 302–17

Goldman, Alvin (2008) *Simulating Minds: The Philosophy, Psychology, and Neuroscience of Mindreading*, Oxford: Oxford University Press

Gordon, Robert (1995) 'Simulation without introspection or inference from me to you', in Martin Davies and Tony Stone, eds, *Mental Simulation: Evaluations and Applications*, Oxford: Blackwell, 53–67

Greenspan, Patricia (1988) *Emotions and Reasons*, London: Routledge

Griswold, Charles (2007) *Forgiveness: A Philosophical Exploration*, Cambridge: Cambridge University Press

Haidt, Jonathan (2001) 'The emotional dog and its rational tail: a social intuitionist approach to moral judgment', *Psychological Review*, 108, 814–34

Harris, Paul (2000) *The Work of the Imagination*, Oxford: Blackwell

Heal, Jane (1995) 'How to think about thinking', in Martin Davies and Tony Stone, eds, *Mental Simulation: Evaluations and Applications*, Oxford: Blackwell, 33–52

Hinckfuss, Ian (1987) *The Moral Society, Its Structure and Effects*, Preprint series in environmental philosophy, Australian National University, no. 16

Holodynski, Manfred and Wolfgang Friedlmeier (2006) *Development of Emotions and Emotion Regulation*, New York: Springer

Jeannerod, M. (1995) 'Mental imagery in the motor context', *Neuropsycholgia* 33(11), 1419–32

Jeffries, Stuart (2002) 'The quest for truth', *The Guardian*, 30 November 2002, *http://www.guardian. co.uk/books/2002/nov/30/academicexperts.higher-education* (accessed 7 January 2013)

Kaster, Robert (2005) *Emotion, Restraint, and Community in Ancient Rome*, Oxford: Oxford University Press

Kekes, John (2005) *The Roots of Evil*, Ithaca, NY: Cornell University Press

Kelly, Daniel (2011) *Yuk: The Nature and Moral Significance of Disgust*, Cambridge, MA: MIT Press

Kind, Amy (2001) 'Putting the image back in imagination', *Philosophy and Phenomenological Research* 62(1), 85–109

Kivy, Peter (1989) *Sound Sentiment: An Essay in the Musical Emotions*, Philadelphia, PA: Temple University Press

Knobe, Joshua (2008) 'The concept of intentional action: a case study in the uses of folk psychology', in Joshua Knobe and Shaun Nichols, eds, *Experimental Philosophy*, Oxford: Oxford University Press, 129–48

Knobe, Joshua and Shaun Nichols, eds (2008) *Experimental Philosophy*, Oxford: Oxford University Press

Kohlberg, Lawrence (1981) *Essays on Moral Development, Vol. I: The Philosophy of Moral Development*, New York: Harper & Row

Lewis, C. S. (1961) *A Grief Observed*, London: Faber & Faber

McGinn, Colin (2004) *Mindsight: Image, Dream, Meaning*, Cambridge, MA: Harvard University Press

References

Maibom, Heidi (2009) 'Feeling for others: empathy, sympathy, and morality', *Inquiry* 52(5), 483–99

Maibom, Heidi (2010) 'The descent of shame', *Philosophy and Phenomenological Research* 80(3), 566–94

Matravers, Derek (2011) 'Empathy as a route to knowledge', in Amy Coplan and Peter Goldie, eds, *Empathy: Philosophical and Psychological Perspectives*, Oxford: Oxford University Press, 19–30

Moeller, Hans-Georg (2009) *The Moral Fool: A Case for Amorality*, New York: Columbia University Press

Morton, Adam (1996) 'The disunity of the moral', in Jan Bransen and Marc Slors, eds, *The Problematic Reality of Values*, Amsterdam: Van Gorcum, 142–55

Morton, Adam (2002a) 'Beware stories: emotions and virtues', in Peter Goldie, ed., *Understanding Emotions*, Farnham: Ashgate, 55–63

Morton, Adam (2002b) 'Emotional accuracy', *Proceedings of the Aristotelian Society*, supplementary vol. 76, 265–75

Morton, Adam (2002c) *The Importance of Being Understood*, London: Routledge

Morton, Adam (2004) *On Evil*, London: Routledge

Morton, Adam (2006) 'Imagination and misimagination', in Shaun Nichols, ed., *The Architecture of the Imagination: New Essays on Pretense, Possibility, and Fiction*, Oxford University Press, 57–72

Morton, Adam (2009a) 'Folk psychology', in Brian McLaughlin, Ansgar Beckermann, and Sven Walter, eds, *The Oxford Handbook of Philosophy of Mind*, New York: Oxford University Press, 713–26

Morton, Adam (2009b) 'Good citizens and moral heroes', in Pedro Tabensky, ed., *The Positive Function of Evil*, Basingstoke: Palgrave, 127–38

Morton, Adam (2010a) 'Emotion, virtue, and knowledge', in Peter Goldie, ed., *The Oxford Companion to Philosophy of Emotion*, Oxford: Oxford University Press, 385–400

Morton, Adam (2010b) 'Imagining evil', *Ateliers de l'éthique* 5(1), *http://www.creum.umontreal.ca/spip.php?article1171* (accessed 7 January 2013)

Morton, Adam (2011) 'Empathy for the devil', in Amy Coplan and Peter Goldie, eds, *Empathy: Philosophical and Psychological Perspectives*, Oxford: Oxford University Press, 318–30

Nichols, Shaun (2004) *Sentimental Rules*, Oxford: Oxford University Press

Nichols, Shaun and Stephen Stich (2003) *Mindreading: An Integrated Account of Pretence, Self-Awareness, and Understanding of Other Minds*, Oxford: Oxford University Press

Nisbett, Richard E. and Lee Ross (1980) *Human Inference: Strategies and Shortcomings of Social Judgement*, Englewood Cliffs, NJ: Prentice Hall

Nussbaum, Martha (2001) *Upheavals of Thought: The Intelligence of Emotions*, Cambridge: Cambridge University Press

Prinz, Jesse (2007) *The Emotional Construction of Morals*, Oxford: Oxford University Press

Ratcliffe, Matthew (2008) *Feelings of Being*, Oxford: Oxford University Press

Robinson, Jenefer (2010) 'Emotional responses to music: what are they? how do they work? and are they relevant to aesthetic appreciation?', in Peter

Goldie, ed., *The Oxford Companion to Philosophy of Emotion*, Oxford: Oxford University Press, 651–80

Rorty, Amelie Oksenberg (1980) 'Agent regret', in Amelie Oksenberg Rorty, ed., *Explaining Emotions*, Berkeley: University of California Press, 489–506

Rorty, Amelie Oksenberg (1982) 'From passions to emotions and sentiments', *Philosophy* 57, 159–72

Sang-hun, Choe (2012) 'A monk's earthly mission: Easing North Korean's pain', *New York Times*, 27 April, *http://www.nytimes.com/2012/04/28/world/asia/venerable-pomnyuns-earthly-mission-is-to-aid-north-korea.html?pagewanted=all&_r=0* (accessed 7 January 2013)

Schmitt, Frederick and Reza Lahroodi (2008) 'The epistemic value of curiosity', *Educational Theory* 58, 125–48

Schmitter, Amy (2013) 'The passions: taxonomy and terminology', in James Harris, ed., *The Oxford Handbook of British Philosophy in the Eighteenth Century*, Oxford: Oxford University Press

Schwitzgebel, Eric (2009) 'Do ethicists steal more books?', *Philosophical Psychology* 22(6), 711–25

Schwitzgebel, Eric and Joshua Rust (2009) 'The moral behaviour of ethicists: peer opinion', *Mind* 118(472), 1043–59

Shaver, Philip R., Shelley Wu, and Judith C. Schwartz (1992) 'Cross-cultural similarities and differences in emotion and its representation: a prototype approach', *Review of Personality and Social Psychology* (Special Issue: 'Emotion', ed. Margaret S. Clark) 13, 175–212

Sherman, Nancy (2005) *Stoic Warriors: The Ancient Philosophy behind the Military Mind*, Oxford: Oxford University Press

References

Sherman, Nancy (2011) 'The moral logic of survivor guilt', *New York Times*, 3 July 2011, *http://opinionat or.blogs.nytimes.com/2011/07/03/war-and-the-moral-logic-of-survivor-guilt/* (accessed 7 January 2013)

Soloman, Robert (1993) *The Passions: Emotions and the Meaning of Life*, Indianapolis, IN: Hackett

Sperber, Dan (1996) *Explaining Culture*, Oxford: Wiley-Blackwell

Steuber, Karsten (2006) *Rediscovering Empathy*, Cambridge, MA: MIT Press

Stocker, Michael (2004) 'Some considerations about intellectual desire and emotions', in Robert Solomon, ed., *Thinking about Feeling*, Oxford: Oxford University Press, 130–50

Tappolet, Christine (2000) *Emotions et valeurs*, Paris: Presses Universitaires de France

Tappolet, Christine (2010) 'Emotion, motivation, and action: the case of fear', in Peter Goldie, ed., *The Oxford Companion to Philosophy of Emotion*, Oxford: Oxford University Press, 325–48

Tappolet, Christine (2011) 'Les mauvaises émotions', in Christine Tappolet, Fabrice Teroni, and Anita Konzelmann Ziv, eds, *Les ombres de l'âme: penser les émotions negatives*, Geneva: Markus Haller, 37–54

Taylor, Gabriele (1985) *Pride, Shame, and Guilt: Emotions of Self-Assessment*, Oxford: Oxford University Press

Vorauer, Jacquie and Stacey Sasaki (2009) '"Helpful only in the abstract?": Ironic effects of empathy in intergroup interaction', *Psychological Science* 20(2), 191–7

Walton, Kendal (1990) *Mimesis as Make-Believe*, Cambridge, MA: Harvard University Press

Walton, Kendal (2006) 'On the (so-called) puzzle of imaginative resistance', in Shaun Nichols, ed., *The Architecture of the Imagination: New Essays on Pretense, Possibility, and Fiction*, Oxford: Oxford University Press, 137–48

Williams, Bernard (1973) 'Ethical consistency', in *Problems of the Self: Philosophical Papers 1956–1972*, Cambridge: Cambridge University Press, 166–86

Williams, Bernard (1981) 'Moral luck', in *Moral Luck*, Cambridge: Cambridge University Press, 20–39

Williams, Bernard (1985) *Ethics and the Limits of Philosophy*, London: Fontana

Williams, Bernard (1993) *Shame and Necessity*, Berkeley: University of California Press

Williamson, Timothy (2007) *The Philosophy of Philosophy*, Oxford: Blackwell

Wood, James (2009) *How Fiction Works*, New York: Vintage

Zagzebski, Linda (2003) 'Emotion and moral judgment', *Philosophy and Phenomenological Research* 66(1), 104–24

Zaki, Jamil, Niall Bolger, and Kevin Ochsner (2009) 'Unpacking the informational bases of empathic accuracy', *Emotion* 9(4), 478–87

Zimmerman, Michael (1993) 'A plea for ambivalence', *Metaphilosophy* 24, 382–9

Index

Index